YORK NOTES

General Editors: Professor A.N. Jeffares (*University of Stirling*) & Professor Suheil Bushrui (*American University of Beirut*)

William Shakespeare

MUCH ADO ABOUT NOTHING

Notes by John Drakakis

BA MA (CARDIFF) DIP ED (EXETER)
Lecturer in English Studies, University of Stirling

LONGMAN
YORK PRESS

Acknowledgement
The illustrations of The Globe Theatre are from *The Globe Restored in Theatre: A Way of Seeing* by C. Walter Hodges, published by Oxford University Press.
© Oxford University Press

YORK PRESS
Immeuble Esseily, Place Riad Solh, Beirut.

LONGMAN GROUP UK LIMITED
Longman House, Burnt Mill, Harlow,
Essex CM20 2JE, England
Associated companies, branches and representatives
throughout the world

© Librairie du Liban 1980

First published 1980
Fifth impression 1991

ISBN 0-582-02288-6

Produced by Longman Group (FE) Ltd.
Printed in Hong Kong

Contents

Part 1: Introduction   *page* 5

The life of William Shakespeare   5

The Elizabethan theatre   8

The sources of *Much Ado About Nothing*   13

A note on the text   14

Part 2: Summaries   16

A general summary   16

Detailed summaries   16

Part 3: Commentary   68

Themes   69

The plots   75

Setting   77

Character and characterisation   79

The language of *Much Ado About Nothing*   103

Scenes and structure   105

Part 4: Hints for study   109

Essay questions and revision   110

Answering questions   111

Part 5: Suggestions for further reading   116

The author of these notes   117

Part 1

Introduction

The life of William Shakespeare

William Shakespeare was born in Stratford-upon-Avon, a small town in Warwickshire. He was christened in Holy Trinity Church on 26 April 1564, and patriotic enthusiasts, eager to have his birth coincide with the celebration of St George's day (St George is the patron-saint of the English) have suggested that he was born on 23 April 1564. Shakespeare's father, John, had married Mary Arden, the daughter of a local landowner from the village of Wilmcote to the north-west of Stratford, and by 1564 he had built a successful business as a glover and merchant. He bought land and houses in Stratford, and in 1568 he was made Mayor. But after 1575 his fortunes declined and he was forced to mortgage some of his property in order to pay his debts.

Little is known of Shakespeare's early life. He probably attended the King's New School in Stratford and in 1582, at the age of eighteen, he married Anne Hathaway, the daughter of a farmer who lived in the small village of Shottery not far from Stratford. Anne was some seven years older than her husband. On 26 May 1583 Shakespeare's eldest daughter, Susanna, was christened, and some eighteen months later, on 2 February, his twin children Hamnet and Judith were christened.

The years 1585–1592 are usually described by biographers of Shakespeare as 'the Lost Years' since nothing is known about this period of his life. He may have become a schoolmaster for part of this time, and he may have been arrested for poaching. These are speculations based on hearsay evidence, but it was sometime during these years that he left Stratford for London and for a career in the theatre. Periodically companies of touring players passed through Stratford, and it is possible that Shakespeare joined one of them. We know that in 1587, one such company, The Queen's Men, was short of an actor, although we have no certain evidence that the person they recruited was indeed Shakespeare.

The first reference to Shakespeare the professional dramatist occurs in 1592 when the writer and dramatist Robert Greene referred to him disparagingly as 'an upstart crow' who was 'in his own conceit the only Shake-scene in a country'. By this time Shakespeare had already written the *Henry VI* plays (from which Greene had quoted in his insulting remarks). In 1593 the narrative poem *Venus and Adonis* was published, and it was dedicated to Henry Wriothesley, the third Earl of Southampton. In 1594 another narrative poem, *The Rape of Lucrece*, was published and dedicated to the same person. It was also probably during the period 1592–4 when the London theatres were closed because of the outbreaks of the plague, that many of the sonnets were written, and some commentators have suggested that Wriothesley is the mysterious 'Mr W.H.' to whom they were dedicated when they were published in 1609.

By 1594 Shakespeare was a member of the company of actors known as The Lord Chamberlain's Men, which numbered among its ranks actors such as the Clown William Kempe, and the famous Richard Burbage. We know too that in addition to writing plays for this company Shakespeare also acted himself. For example, he acted in Ben Jonson's comedy *Every Man in His Humour* in 1598, a play he was to remember when he came to write *Othello*, and later in Jonson's *Sejanus* (1603) where he may have played the part of the Emperor Tiberius. It has been suggested that he played the roles of Adam in *As You Like It* (1598–9) and the Ghost in *Hamlet* (1600–1).

The regular playhouse of the Lord Chamberlain's Men was the Theatre, situated in Shoreditch outside the northern boundaries of the City of London, which had been built by Cuthbert and Richard Burbage in 1576, long before Shakespeare arrived in London. In 1598 this playhouse was dismantled and its timbers taken across to Southwark on the south bank of the River Thames to be used in the building of the Globe Theatre. This is the theatre with which we most associate Shakespeare, and the dramatist himself became a sharer in the new enterprise, thus becoming entitled to receive ten per cent of the profits.

Meanwhile, Shakespeare had already begun to invest the money he was earning as a dramatist. In 1597 he was wealthy enough to buy the house known as New Place, the second biggest house in Stratford. This was the first of a number of purchases of land which he made during the period 1597–1605, and the records of his various business dealings in Stratford still survive. In 1596, and at the age of eleven, his son Hamnet died, while in 1601 his father John also died. In 1607 his eldest daughter Susanna married John Hall, and they lived for some time in the cottage now known as Hall's Croft (which currently houses the Stratford Festival Club). After Shakespeare's death in 1616 the Halls moved into New Place.

By 1603, when Queen Elizabeth died, Shakespeare had written some twenty-four plays, and the Chamberlain's Men had become the leading acting company of the time. Indeed, it has been suggested that the play *The Merry Wives of Windsor* (1600) was written at the request of Elizabeth herself. *Much Ado About Nothing* was written some time between 1598 and 1600 when it first appeared in print in a quarto version. It is one of the so-called 'mature' comedies, and is usually grouped with *As You Like It*, *The Merry Wives of Windsor*, and *Twelfth Night*, the comedies which Shakespeare wrote immediately before embarking on the major tragedies. During the period 1600–8 Shakespeare wrote the major tragedies, beginning with *Hamlet* (1600–1), and ending with *Coriolanus* (1607–8), but he obviously remembered certain features of *Much Ado About Nothing* when in 1604 he came to write *Othello*, and he returned to the central theme once more in 1610 when he came to write *The Winter's Tale*.

In 1608, Shakespeare, along with his business associates the Burbages, John Heminges and Henry Condell (who later jointly edited the First Folio of Shakespeare's plays in 1623), Thomas Evans, and William Sly, leased a small indoor theatre in the City of London called Blackfriars. Some critics have felt that this new building, different in its structure from the Globe, played a large part in the noticeable alteration of Shakespeare's dramatic style at this time. It is argued that *Pericles* (1607–8), *Cymbeline* (1609), *The Winter's Tale* (1610), and *The Tempest* (1611) are the result of Shakespeare's artistic response to a new and more intimate kind of theatre. Unfortunately this argument does not hold, since the first record of a performance of *The Winter's Tale* in 1611 intimates that it took place at the Globe. Also, one of Shakespeare's very last plays, *Henry VIII*, was performed at the Globe since during an actual performance the firing of a cannon set the theatre alight and it burned to the ground.

After 1613 Shakespeare seems to have written no more plays. His last few years were spent in retirement in Stratford, where he died on 23 April 1616. Popular legend has it that Shakespeare caught a fever after a drinking bout with Ben Jonson and the poet Michael Drayton. Unfortunately, we do not know the circumstances of his death, but his will survives, and biographers have sought to infer much from its contents. For example, the bequest of his 'second best bed with the furniture' to his widow Anne has prompted speculation about matrimonial disharmony in the Shakespeare household. But his latest, and possibly most reliable biographer, Professor Samuel Schoenbaum, has suggested* that in any event Anne would have been entitled to one third of Shakespeare's estate, and that the bed may well have had sentimental associations. It seems more than likely that the best bed was reserved for visitors to New Place.

In 1623, some seven years after Shakespeare's death, two of his former partners John Heminges and Henry Condell gathered together his plays in one impressive volume, known as the First Folio. Of the thirty-five plays in it, some sixteen had never been printed before.

William Shakespeare: A compact Documentary Life, Oxford University Press, 1977.

The Elizabethan theatre

Shakespeare was a professional dramatist, and his life therefore revolved very much around the public theatre of his day. In order to understand how his plays work on the stage, we need to have some idea of the kind of theatre for which they were originally written. The Prologue in Shakespeare's history play *Henry V* (1599–1600) tells us what actors and dramatist expected in the way of cooperation from their audiences; spectators are urged to:

> *Piece out our imperfections with your thoughts:*
> *Into a thousand parts divide one man,*
> *And make imaginary puissance;*
> *Think when we talk of horses that you see them*
> *Printing their proud hooves i'the receiving earth;*
> *For 'tis your thoughts that now must deck our kings,*
> *Carry them here and there, jumping o'er times,*
> *Turning the accomplishment of many years*
> *Into an hour-glass;*
> (Prologue, lines 23–31)

What kind of theatre could permit so complete an engagement of the imagination? Let us begin by looking at the physical measurements of such a building. The builder's contract for the Fortune Theatre, which was erected outside the northern boundary of the city of London in the parish of St Giles in Cripplegate in 1600, still survives, and is fairly exact in its information. Though the Fortune was a square building, it was modelled in certain crucial respects upon Shakespeare's own theatre, the Globe, and was erected by the same builder, Peter Streete. It contained a rectangular stage which jutted out into 'the yard' of the theatre, and measured 27½ feet deep by 43 feet wide, similar to that of the Globe. We usually refer to this type of theatre as 'theatre-in-the-round'. In both theatres the 'yard' was open to the sky, providing standing room for part of the audience, while the remainder sat in the more expensive but covered galleries set in the outer walls of the building. The stage itself was covered by a large canopy supported by two stout pillars, and was usually referred to as 'the Heavens'. On the underside of the Heavens (that is, its ceiling) were probably painted the signs of the zodiac, and the entire cosmological layout of the Universe as the Elizabethans understood it. Clearly, Heaven and its position in the Universe was not left to the imagination of the audience. Similarly, because the stage stood about four feet off the ground, there was a place for Heaven's opposite, 'Hell', which was usually reached through a trap-door in the floor of the stage. Thus, the stage itself could represent, on the one hand, the Universe and man's struggle within it with the forces of good and evil, which was the stuff of tragedy, or it could, on the other hand, represent 'society' and its attendant moral virtues and vices, normally the subject of comedy.

The actors made their entrances and their exits through one of a number of doors situated at the back of the stage. It seems likely that at stage level there were two small doors—one each side of the stage—and a large pair of double-doors in the centre of the back wall of the stage which, when opened, could be used as an 'inner stage'. It was at the back, and behind these doors, in what is called the 'tiring-

THE GLOBE PLAYHOUSE

The theatre, originally built by James Burbage in 1576, was made of wood (Burbage had been trained as a carpenter). It was situated to the north of the River Thames on Shoreditch in Finsbury Fields. There was trouble with the lease of the land, and so the theatre was dismantled in 1598, and reconstructed 'in an other forme' on the south side of the Thames as the Globe. Its sign is thought to have been a figure of the Greek hero Hercules carrying the globe. It was built in six months, its galleries being roofed with thatch. This caught fire in 1613 when some smouldering wadding, from a cannon used in a performance of Shakespeare's *Henry VIII*, lodged in it. The theatre was burnt down, and when it was rebuilt again on the old foundations, the galleries were roofed with tiles.

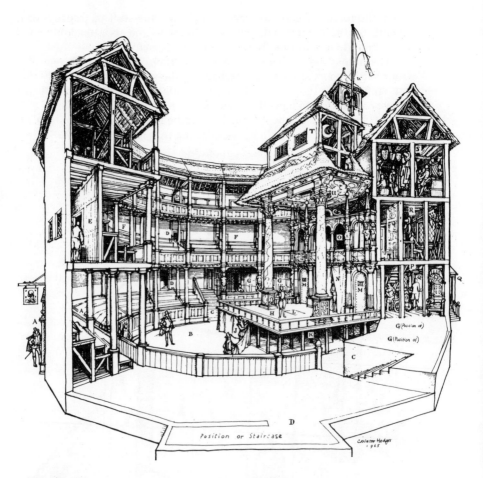

A CONJECTURAL RECONSTRUCTION OF THE INTERIOR OF
THE GLOBE PLAYHOUSE

AA Main entrance
 B The Yard
CC Entrances to lowest gallery
 D Entrance to staircase and upper galleries
 E Corridor serving the different sections of the
   middle gallery
 F Middle gallery ('Twopenny Rooms')
 G 'Gentlemen's Rooms or Lords Rooms'
 H The stage
 J The hanging being put up round the stage
 K The 'Hell' under the stage
 L The stage trap, leading down to the Hell
MM Stage doors

 N Curtained 'place behind the stage'
 O Gallery above the stage, used as required
   sometimes by musicians, sometimes by
   spectators, and often as part of the play
 P Back-stage area (the tiring-house)
 Q Tiring-house door
 R Dressing-rooms
 S Wardrobe and storage
 T The hut housing the machine for lowering
   enthroned gods, etc., to the stage
 U The 'Heavens'
 W Hoisting the playhouse flag

house', that the actors changed their costumes, or kept their stage properties. Above the tiring-house was a balcony which was often used in particular scenes; for example, if the gulling of Claudio and Don Pedro in *Much Ado About Nothing* had been played on stage and not merely reported, then the disguised Margaret would have been positioned somewhere on the balcony above the tiring-house, as seems to be clear from Borachio's description of the episode:

> but know that I have tonight wooed Margaret, the Lady Hero's gentlewoman, by the name of Hero; she leans me out at her mistress' chamber-window, bids me a thousand times good-night—I tell this tale vilely—I should first tell thee how the Prince, Claudio, and my master, planted, and placed, and possessed by my master Don John, saw afar off in the orchard this amiable encounter.
>
> (III.3.139–46)

Also, there were no artificial lights in the Elizabethan theatre, and so performances took place in the afternoons. The 'tapers' carried by Claudio, Don Pedro, and Balthazar in Act V, Scene 3 help to reinforce the illusion that the action is taking place at night, although they are also part of a larger impression which this scene seeks to create, that of a visual darkness preceding the final illumination of the truth which comes with the day itself. Moreover, there is a sense in which both Claudio and Don Pedro are being 'kept in the dark' about Hero's fate, a darkness which symbolises ignorance, as well as being the time when deception and evil deeds occur. In this way the physical setting is made to support and reinforce the development of the play's themes.

Unfortunately we know far too little about how actors moved and spoke on the stage, although we may safely assume that they did so in ways different from those of modern actors. We should also bear in mind that there were no actresses on the Elizabethan stage; the parts of women were played by highly trained young boys whose voices had not yet broken. Thus the parts of Beatrice, Hero, and Margaret, for example, would have been played by boys, and an Elizabethan audience would have accepted this convention. Also, the stage contained no fixed scenery, and no attempt was made to create the 'illusion' that everyday events were taking place. As the Prologue to *Henry V* suggests, it was the audience which provided, through its own corporate imagination, the 'setting' or background against which the action took place. In the case of Tragedy, the 'localised' settings for particular parts of the action must have been viewed in relation to the universal setting (Man acting out the drama of his own destiny between the opposed forces of 'Heaven' and 'Hell'), of which the theatre itself was the supreme symbol. In the case of Comedy the universal setting was implied, while the stage itself represented 'all the world' with its confusions, complications, paradoxes, and resolutions. Indeed, it was not for nothing that Shakespeare's company called their theatre the Globe. This absence of fixed scenery meant that the language of the play became the focus of the audience's attention, since in addition to communicating the states of mind of particular characters, it also provided details of these 'localised' settings. Benedick's 'In my chamber-window lies a book; bring it hither to me in the orchard.' (II.3.3–4), is in this context a kind of stage direction, designed to tell the audience where he is, and it establishes 'the orchard' as the setting for each of the succeeding deceptions which take place later in the play. Leonato's 'Marry, thou dost wrong me, thou dissembler, thou:–/Nay, never lay thy hand upon thy sword;' (V.1.54–5) both describes Claudio's gesture, and its meaning, on the one hand, but it also reinforces a major theme in the play whereby 'appearance' is often at odds with 'reality', on the other, as Claudio's reply indicates: 'In faith, my hand meant nothing to my sword.' (V.1.58).

Details of this kind are scattered throughout the play, and they help us to 'place' the action as well as guide our responses to the ways in which particular characters behave and speak. The sheer artificiality of the edifice of the play meant that it was not considered necessary to imitate closely the language of everyday speech. The intensity and concentration of expression could be varied to suit the requirements of each situation. For example, the early wit combats between Beatrice and Benedick are in lively prose, while after his change of heart Benedick's utterance becomes more formal. On the other hand, much of what Claudio says is in blank verse, indicating his 'romantic' inclinations, and helping to sustain a broader contrast between his relationship with Hero, and that between Benedick and Beatrice.

The Elizabethan theatre was an intimate theatre (for example, no spectator was more than about 60 feet from the stage) despite the fact that a playhouse like the Globe could hold an audience of between two and three thousand people. Because there was no attempt to think in terms of a 'picture-frame', which is a feature of the modern proscenium-arch stage, the large acting area could be quickly transformed from one locality to another. Thus the action was continuous throughout, and the movement from scene to scene resembles in its speed that of the modern film, or even the radio play, capable of moving wherever the requirements of the action dictate. In addition to these physical characteristics, Shakespeare was perhaps more fortunate than some of his fellow dramatists in that from about 1594 onwards when he joined the company known as the Chamberlain's Men, he was able to write for specific actors whose talents and potential skills he knew intimately. For example, a stage direction in the original quarto version of 1600 of *Much Ado About Nothing* refers to Kempe, the Will Kempe who up to 1599 was the resident Clown with Shakespeare's company, and who played the part of Dogberry. Another actor, Richard Cowley, whose name appears along with Kempe's in the stage directions of the quarto of 1600, was the actor who played the part of Verges. This relationship with his actors was sustained throughout Shakespeare's working life, and represents possibly the most fruitful cooperation of playwright, actors, and theatre in the history of English drama.

The sources of *Much Ado About Nothing*

Although a number of versions of the story were extant at the time, three major sources have been identified for the Claudio-Hero plot in *Much Ado About Nothing*. The parallel plot involving Beatrice and Benedick, along with the scenes involving Dogberry, Verges, and The Watch, are all thought to be Shakespeare's own invention. One version of the Claudio-Hero story is to be found in Book 5 of the long narrative poem *Orlando Furioso*, written by the Italian poet Ludovico Ariosto (1474-1533); it was first published in Italy in 1516, and appeared in English in a translation by Sir John Harrington in 1591, some seven years before Shakespeare's play.

A second source is the story of Phedon and Philemon in Book 2 of Edmund Spenser's *The Faerie Queene*, another long narrative poem, published in 1596. Much of Spenser's poem is intricately allegorical and the Phedon-Philemon episode is no exception. The wandering knight Sir Guyon comes across a squire who is being savagely beaten by the madman Furor, while the Hag Occasion looks on. Sir Guyon rescues the squire who tells him that he has been the victim of his trusted friend Philemon's deceit. Philemon had deceived Phedon into thinking that his mistress Claribella, whom he was about to marry, had been unfaithful to him. With the aid of her maid Pryene, Philemon had staged a scene designed to convince Phedon of Claribella's infidelity, and once having been convinced, the squire kills his mistress in a rage. But when he realises his mistake, he seeks further revenge upon Pryene and Philemon. He catches Philemon and poisons him and is hotly in pursuit of Pryene when he encounters Furor and his accomplice Occasion.

The third major source is the twentieth story from the *Novelle* of Matteo Bandello (*c. 1480–1562*) first published in Italy in 1554, and translated into French 1582 in Belleforest's *Histoires Tragiques*. The location of Bandello's story is Messina, as in Shakespeare's play, and the lady Fenicia's father's name is Lionato di' Lionati. In Bandello's story Sir Timbreo (Shakespeare's Claudio) engages a matchmaker to arrange a marriage between himself and the young Fenicia. But another knight of Messina, Sir Girondo, is also in love with Fenicia, and seeks to poison the relationship between her and Sir Timbreo. A scene is arranged where Sir Timbreo can obtain 'proof' of Fenicia's infidelity, and when he is convinced he sends word to her father that he will not marry her. When Fenicia is accused she faints, goes into a coma, and is thought by her relatives to be dead, but while they are washing her body in preparation for burial, she revives. Lionato decides to go through with a mock funeral, and to get her away to the country so that when she is older, and cannot be recognised, she may then be safely married off. Lionato's brother Girolamo (Shakespeare's Antonio) takes her away to the country, but Sir Girondo confesses his treachery both to Sir Timbreo and to Lionato. Sir Timbreo then puts himself completely into Lionato's power, and agrees not to marry without his consent or approval. A year passes, and Lionato arranges for him to marry a much-changed Fenicia (she is now seventeen, and has changed her name to Lucilla). Only after the marriage is Fenicia's true identity revealed, since she has changed so much that even Sir Timbreo does not recognise her. Sir Girondo is not disappointed either, since Lionato has a second daughter, Belfiore, who is offered to him as a wife, converting the evil he tried to do into good.

A note on the text

As a professional dramatist Shakespeare's primary concern was to write plays for performance by actors whose skills he knew well. Consequently, he seems to have shown little personal inclination or concern to oversee the publication of his plays in book form, although there is some evidence to show that publication was occasionally sanctioned by the theatre company for which he worked. Even so, nearly half the plays which comprise the First Folio of 1623 had not appeared in print during his lifetime, while in the case of some (*Hamlet,* and *Othello,* for example) the earlier quarto texts differ significantly from their Folio counterparts. Textual bibliographers have sought to account for these differences in a variety of ways, through the investigation of the peculiar habits of the printers who printed the plays, and through seeking to trace the original manuscript sources which printers may have used.

Much Ado About Nothing is no exception to this general tendency, although the textual problems raised by the play are not as great as they are in the two other cases mentioned. It was first published in quarto in 1600, and there are a number of minor differences between this and the Folio text of the play which appeared in 1623. Scholars are generally agreed that the quarto was printed from Shakespeare's own manuscript, and that the Folio version was substantially a reprint of the 1600 quarto. Thus, all modern editions of the play rely upon the quarto of 1600 for their texts. The quarto is of some interest since it is generally thought to contain the sorts of blemishes to be found in play manuscripts generally of this period. For example, the very first stage direction refers to 'Innogen' the wife of Leonato, who appears onstage here, and at the beginning of Act II, Scene 1, but who in both cases is given nothing to say. J. Dover Wilson, in his Cambridge edition of the play, offers the generally held view that Shakespeare was using as his source an old play, and that in revising it for performance, he had included a character for whom he had no plans in his revision.* The quarto contains a number of confusions of this sort in stage directions and speech headings.

One interesting error concerns the substitution of actors' names for those of the characters they represented; for example, at the beginning of Act IV, Scene 2, Dogberry's line: 'Yea, marry, let them come before me.' (IV.2.9) is ascribed to 'Kemp', the resident Clown, Will Kempe, for whom the part had been especially written. Similarly, later in the same scene, Verges's line: 'Let them be in the hands–' (IV.2.66) is ascribed to 'Couly', the Richard Cowley who played the part. These are understandable substitutions, and suggest that Shakespeare conceived these parts with particular actors in mind. If the source of the quarto is, indeed, the author's manuscript, as many believe, then errors of this sort which it contains, offer a glimpse of a dramatist working under the sort of creative pressure which the task of providing plays for a successful company to act forced upon him.

*Much Ado About Nothing, ed. J. Dover Wilson, Cambridge University Press, Cambridge, 1923, pp. 89–108.

Part 2

Summaries
of MUCH ADO ABOUT NOTHING

A general summary

Much Ado About Nothing is basically about two groups of lovers who are deceived in various ways by those about them. Claudio's love for Hero is thwarted by the evil designs of the villainous Don John who is jealous of the younger man's achievement. Consequently, Claudio rejects Hero at the wedding ceremony itself, because he has been persuaded that she has been unfaithful to him. Benedick and Beatrice, on the other hand, seem not to be initially attracted to each other but are deceived by Claudio and Don Pedro, with the aid of others, into believing that each has some affection for the other. Ironically, the plot to bring Beatrice and Benedick together, which is laudable in its intentions, is carried out by the very characters who themselves fall victim to a far more devastating deception perpetrated by Don John.

The potential seriousness of Don John's plot is not, however, allowed to upset the comic balance of the play, since a group of minor characters, Dogberry, Verges, and the Watch, who are charged with preserving Law and Order in Messina, overhear Conrade and Borachio discussing Don John's plan even before it has been carried out. Because of their amusing incompetence, they are unable to reveal this information in time to prevent Claudio from publicly disgracing Hero in the church, but eventually the true story about Don John's deception of Claudio and Don Pedro comes to light. Thanks to the care and planning of Friar Francis, the revelation of the truth makes possible the reuniting of Claudio and Hero, and this takes place just at the point when Benedick and Beatrice decide that they too are finally prepared to relinquish their earlier opposition to marriage. With both couples safely united, and with Don John's villainy finally exposed, the obstacles are forgotten in a final dance of celebration.

Detailed summaries

Act I Scene 1

The play opens outside the house of Leonato, the Governor of Messina, who is reading a letter which a Messenger has just delivered to him. His daughter Hero and her cousin Beatrice look on, and he reveals that Don Pedro of Arragon will be arriving shortly in Messina. Don Pedro has won a military victory, but a young Florentine, Claudio, whose uncle lives in Messina, has also distinguished himself in the battle. Leonato believes that Claudio's uncle will be happy to hear the news of his nephew's success, but the Messenger replies that he has already been told. Though overjoyed to hear the news, Claudio's uncle had responded by bursting into tears, a gesture the paradoxical significance of which does not escape the attention of the Messenger, since weeping is both a sign of happiness and 'a badge of bitterness'. Leonato takes a rather different view, suggesting that such a gesture reveals a nature which is both kind and honest. This light-hearted difference of opinion gently introduces the theme of disguise which will be developed later in the play.

The dialogue becomes a little more lighthearted with Beatrice's enquiry after a certain 'Signior Mountanto'. Her request confuses the Messenger who knows nobody of that name, but Hero reveals that Beatrice is really enquiring after 'Signior Benedick of Padua'. When she hears that Benedick has also distinguished himself in the battle, she immediately seeks to belittle his achievement, so that Leonato is forced to explain to the Messenger that she and Benedick are involved in 'a kind of merry war' with each other. We are, perhaps, a little suspicious from the outset that Beatrice's harsh criticisms of Benedick may well disguise a deeper affection for him, especially when we reflect that it is she who asks about him in the first place. But, for the moment, the picture she paints of her adversary is one of an inconstant man, intellectually limited, a follower of fashion, and a corrupter of those with whom he comes into close contact. This scathing attack serves also to indicate that Beatrice does not think that she herself is likely to be taken in either by appearances, or by the attractions of romance. She wishes, from the outset, to establish herself as a 'realist', judging those around her in the harsh light of experience, but Beatrice's conception of herself will prove a source of comic irony later in the play.

With the entry of Don Pedro, Claudio, Benedick, Balthazar, and Don John the Bastard brother of Don Pedro, the emphasis moves away from the harsh realism of Beatrice's comments to the romantic grandeur surrounding their victory. But just as the Messenger's and Leonato's courtesies were earlier undercut by Beatrice's harsh comments, so now Benedick seeks to undermine the courtesies which Don Pedro exchanges with Leonato. Although Leonato checks Benedick's frivolity, this interruption provides the opportunity for a response from Beatrice, and it is their war of words which now occupies our attention. Each tries to overcome the other with insults, although on this occasion it is Benedick who emerges as the victor with his allegation that Beatrice's distinguishing feature is the speed of her tongue. Thus he strongly implies that her words are without substance, balancing Beatrice's earlier remark that he was a man of 'appearances' only. There follows the courtly dialogue of Leonato and Don Pedro, with the latter promising to remain in Messina for a month. Leonato extends his welcome to the sinister figure of Don John, who is, by his own admission, a man of few words, and he leaves with his guests, followed by all except Claudio and Benedick.

Claudio asks Benedick if he noticed Leonato's daughter, Hero, but the response he gets is both frivolous and equivocal. Don Pedro returns, wondering why Claudio and Benedick did not follow on to Leonato's house, and is told that the reason is Claudio's attraction to Hero. This meets with his full approval, though Benedick returns to the subject of his general hatred of women and vows he will remain a bachelor. The scepticism which this arouses in Don Pedro suggests that this promise will shortly come under attack. In the meantime, Benedick is asked to go and confirm Don Pedro's acceptance of Leonato's invitation to supper, and he leaves, the victim of mild ridicule from the other two.

The flexible, witty prose of the earlier dialogue now gives way to one which is both formal and in verse, as Don Pedro and Claudio discuss the latter's affection for Hero. This dialogue establishes Claudio as a 'romantic' character, and initiates a plot whereby Don Pedro offers to approach both Leonato and Hero on his behalf. He plans to disguise himself as Claudio, and to reveal his love to Hero at the forthcoming celebrations. This is the second of two potential plot-strands that are contained in the opening scene of the play. Firstly, the foundations are laid for conflict and reversal in the relationship between Benedick and Beatrice, and secondly, a step is taken to consolidate the relationship between Claudio and Hero.

NOTES AND GLOSSARY

by this:	according to the information which this letter contains
three leagues:	a distance of approximately nine miles (a league was three miles)
action:	battle
name:	reputation
equally remembered:	rewarded with equal measure
figure:	outward appearance (This is the first of a number of references in this scene to an implied discrepancy between outward 'appearance' and the 'inner' man)
feats:	achievements
better ... expectation:	fulfilled more than anyone expected of him
badge:	sign (usually referred to the crest of arms worn by a servant on the sleeve of his left arm)
In ... measure:	in large quantity

kind:	natural
truer:	more honest or sincere
so washed:	washed with tears
Mountanto:	an upward stroke in fencing, and hence a duellist (but Benedick's main weapon, like Beatrice's, is his tongue)
none . . . sort:	nobody in the army of that rank
set . . . bills:	issue public challenges
Cupid:	the God of Love, who is blind, but who pierces the hearts of lovers with arrows from his bow
at . . . flight:	to a contest with bow and arrow (Beatrice is referring to Benedick's refusal to fall in love)
fool:	professional clown
subscribed for:	signed on behalf of
bird-bolt:	a blunt-headed arrow used by professional clowns in an inferior kind of archery (this is part of Beatrice's strategy to undermine what she considers to be Benedick's extreme vanity)
I . . . killing:	Beatrice seeks to discredit Benedick by offering to eat all those he has killed in battle, believing all the time that he has killed nobody
Faith:	In faith (an oath)
tax:	censure or criticise
meet:	get even (with a possible quibble on 'meat' following Beatrice's offer to eat all of Benedick's victims)
musty victual:	stale food
holp:	helped
trencher-man:	eating companion (implying that he is a glutton)
stomach:	appetite
too:	also (the Messenger does not seem to detect the ironic tone of Beatrice's comments)
to a lady:	Beatrice takes the Messenger's phrase 'too, lady' and distorts it
stuffed with:	filled with
stuffed man:	model made to look like a man
for:	as for
we . . . mortal:	we are all frail (Beatrice is playfully questioning what the Messenger says about Benedick's 'inner' qualities)
skirmish . . . wit:	battle of wits
gets nothing:	gains nothing
five wits:	common sense, fantasy, imagination, estimation, and memory, all of which comprise the faculties of the mind

halting:	limping
bear ... difference:	accept it as a feature which distinguished him ('difference' is an heraldic term and refers to the addition to a coat of arms designed to distinguish one branch of a family from another)
wealth:	substance
known:	recognised as
new-sworn:	newly pledged to another in friendship
faith:	fidelity or constancy
ever ... block:	always changes according to the latest fashion
not ... books:	not in your good books (you are not favourably disposed towards him)
an:	even if
burn ... study:	burn my books (Beatrice takes the metaphoric meaning of the Messenger literally
squarer:	braggart
most:	most often
pestilence:	plague, or disease generally
taker:	victim (the one who contracts the disease)
presently:	immediately
the Benedick:	Beatrice converts his name into that of the disease itself
ere 'a be:	before he is
hold friends:	take care to remain friends (in view of the harsh treatment which enemies like Benedick receive)
run mad:	fall victim to disease (the 'disease' Leonato refers to is that of falling in love)
hot January:	a contradiction in terms since January is a cold month (this is Beatrice's way of saying 'never')
is approached:	has arrived
your trouble:	the inconvenience to which my visit has put you
encounter:	confront
embrace ... charge:	fulfil your responsibility
for ... child:	it would be childish of you to think so
have ... full:	are fully answered
by this:	from what has just been said
fathers herself:	is so much like her father that there can be no doubt about her parentage
have ... shoulders:	have his aged head on her young shoulders
as ... is:	no matter how much she resembles him
that. ...will:	that you persist in
marks:	takes any notice of
yet living?:	still alive?
meet:	appropriate

convert:	change
her presence:	'Courtesy' like 'Disdain' is personified here
turncoat:	one who changes his appearance
of:	by
only . . . excepted:	except only you
I would:	I wish
else:	otherwise
pernicious suitor:	villainous wooer (but also a possible quibble on 'suitor' as someone who is dressed, referring to Beatrice's earlier criticism of Benedick as a follower of fashion)
cold blood:	lack of impetuosity
humour:	temperament
'scape:	escape
predestinate:	determined beforehand
an 'twere:	even if it were
rare parrot-teacher:	fine chatterer (Beatrice is being accused of uttering words as a parrot does, without understanding them)
a beast . . . yours:	implying that Benedick is also less than human
continuer:	one who has the capacity to carry on
keep . . .ways:	carry on in the same way
a' God's name:	In God's name (an oath)
a jade's trick:	an ill-tempered horse which slips its head out of its collar (alternatively, Beatrice may be referring to Benedick's having unseated her with his argument in the same way that an ill-tempered horse would unseat its rider)
forsworn:	violate your oath
being reconciled:	since you are now friends
owe . . . duty:	I am obliged to you all
Please it:	If you please
note:	notice
looked on:	saw but paid no attention to
their sex:	women generally
methinks:	I think
low:	short
play . . . jack:	play the part of an habitual mocker
hare-finder:	the joke is that Cupid is blind
Vulcan:	the blacksmith of the Gods who, presumably, burned wood, and who therefore could not be a good carpenter
key:	tone or pitch
to . . . song:	in order to continue in the song
an:	if

May ... December:	the month of May heralds the beginning of good weather, whereas December is in the dead of winter
but:	unless
wear....suspicion:	be a jealous husband and wear a cap to hide his cuckold's horns (horns on the head were supposed to be the sign of a husband whose wife had been unfaithful to him)
threescore:	sixty years old
Go to:	Away with you (an exclamation)
print:	mark or imprint
sigh ... Sundays:	have no rest at all (Sunday was traditionally a day of rest, and the idea of 'sighing' on Sundays indicates an interruption of a restful atmosphere)
constrain:	compel
charge:	call upon
allegiance:	duty or obligation
your ... part:	a question you will have to ask yourself
Mark:	Observe or notice
If ... uttered:	Even if I did tell him such a secret he would have revealed it in this way
old tale:	a story in which someone denies the truth of an allegation even though it is true after all
fetch ... in:	cheat me into revealing the truth
By ... troth:	on my honour
two troths:	Benedick has an obligation to both Don Pedro and Claudio
die ... stake:	prepared to suffer burning at the stake for my belief
heretic:	one who deviates from accepted belief
in ... despite of:	scorning
maintain ... part:	sustain his case
force ... will:	by obstinacy as opposed to rational argument
recheat ... forehead:	a cuckold's horns (which Benedick believes to be the fate of all married men)
hang ... baldrick:	hang my hunting horn in an invisible girdle (in other words to take steps to conceal his cuckold's horns)
fine:	conclusion
go ... finer:	move the better
ere:	before
that ever:	that I will ever
get:	obtain
argument:	proof or example
bottle ... cat:	a cat placed in a leather container and hung up for target practice

Adam:	Adam Bell, a famous archer (also the biblical Adam)
try:	test
doth ... yoke:	is subdued
sensible:	full of good sense
vilely painted:	hideously disguised
good horse:	a good horse
horn-mad:	as mad as a bull (but also a suggestion that Benedick may become the victim of his own belief that all married men are cuckolds)
spent ... Venice:	discharged all his arrows in Venice (a city noted for its amorous freedom)
temporise ... hours:	weaken in time
repair:	return
commend ... him:	convey my regards to him
matter:	substance
embassage:	errand
I ... you:	I entrust you (a formal way of ending a letter, which both Claudio and Don Pedro expand in their mocking replies)
tuition:	protection
body:	substance
guarded:	trimmed
basted:	sewn loosely together
old ends:	old-fashioned bits
do ... good:	assist me
to teach:	to be guided by your wisdom
but how:	however you wish
apt:	eager
affect:	have some affection for
went onward:	went forward
ended action:	the military expedition which has now ended
their ... vacant:	have left a vacuum in my thoughts
rooms:	Claudio divides the human mind up into 'rooms' in accordance with the systems of 'memory' which had been inherited from medieval times
tire... words:	lovers traditionally praised their mistresses in words, usually rhymes
break ... her:	broach the subject with her
to ... end:	for this reason
fine:	refined or delicate
minister	supply assistance
complexion:	the lover's face was traditionally pale
salved:	explained or accounted for

what . . . bridge:	why does the bridge have to be
fairest grant:	most appropriate justification
Look what:	Whatever
'Tis once,:	Once for all
fit:	provide
unclasp . . . heart:	open my heart (that is, tell her what I really feel)
break:	broach the subject

Act I Scene 2

Meanwhile, in Leonato's house preparations are being made for the evening's entertainment. Leonato and his brother, Antonio, discuss briefly the arrangements made to provide music for the celebrations, but Antonio has some surprising news for his brother. One of his servants has overheard part of the conversation between Claudio and Don Pedro, and has reported to Antonio that Don Pedro is in love with Hero. He believes that Don Pedro will reveal his love to her at the celebration. Leonato questions the validity of this report, and decides to do nothing until he is more certain that it is true. But in the meantime he proposes to warn Hero in order that she will not be taken aback by the proposal if and when it comes.

NOTES AND GLOSSARY

As . . . them:	depending upon the outcome
cover:	outward appearance
thick-pleached alley:	a thickly wooded pathway
accordant:	in agreement
present . . . top:	take the opportunity
break with:	discuss it with
hold it:	think that it is
withal:	with the report
peradventure:	perhaps
Cousin:	Kinsman
I . . . mercy:	I beg your pardon
have . . . care:	take care

Act I Scene 3

By contrast with the pace, energy, and humour of the opening two scenes, the appearance of Don John the Bastard, and his companion, Conrade, casts a gloomy shadow over the festivities. Don John is discontented by nature, and a character bent on mischief and disruption. Evidently, it was his surliness which had caused an earlier rift between him and his brother, Don Pedro, but now that it has been healed Conrade urges him not to provoke further disharmony. He rejects this advice, preferring a commitment to downright villainy, and he is clearly the disruptive force in the comic action of the play. Borachio enters carrying news of a prospective marriage, and Don John immediately sees a possible opportunity for mischief. Borachio has overheard Claudio and Don Pedro completing their plan, although unlike Antonio's servant, his version of the details is more accurate. Don John is, evidently, jealous of Claudio's newly acquired reputation, and resolves to think upon a plot to thwart his intended marriage.

NOTES AND GLOSSARY

what . . . good-year:	My goodness! (an expletive)
out . . . measure:	disproportionately
measure:	proportion
occasion . . . breeds:	the circumstances which provoke my my sadness
present:	immediate
born . . . Saturn:	saturnine (gloomy or melancholic)
moral:	rational
mortifying:	deadly
jests:	jokes
have stomach:	am hungry
tend on:	wait upon
claw:	flatter
his humour:	when he is in a frame of mind to be flattered
make . . . show:	reveal
without controlment:	freely
stood . . . against:	opposed
ta'en:	taken
take . . . root:	begin to grow
fair weather:	good prospects
frame:	fashion or formulae
canker:	dog-rose (but also 'disease')
fits . . . blood:	suits my temperament (that is as a Bastard)
fashion:	formulate
carriage:	disposition
enfranchised . . . clog:	allowed to walk, but restricted by the control of others
do . . . liking:	do as I pleased
that . . . am:	the person that I am
intelligence:	news
model:	ground-plan
What . . . fool:	what kind of fool is he
Marry:	to be sure (literally, Mary, the name of the Virgin Mary, used as an oath)
right hand:	right-hand man (that is, the man on whom his brother has come to rely)

proper squire:	fine young man (but spoken ironically)
forward March-chick:	precocious young lady
How . . . this?:	How did you find this out?
entertained:	engaged or employed
perfumer:	one employed to fumigate rooms
smoking . . . room:	fumigating a stale-smelling room
comes me:	in comes
sad conference:	serious conversation
whipt me:	nipped (colloquial expression)
arras:	wall-hanging
start-up:	upstart
cross him:	aggravate or thwart him
cheer:	mirth
prove:	determine

Act II Scene 1

After supper, Leonato, Antonio, Hero and Beatrice are involved in a conversation, with Margaret and Ursula standing by. Leonato has noticed that Don John was not at supper, and this provides an opportunity for both Beatrice and Hero to voice their misgivings about him. For Beatrice, the meditation upon Don John's character leads on to a more general speculation about what she believes might be the attributes of her ideal man. Leonato feels that she is too critical, but she responds by rejecting the prospect of any husband at all. Like Benedick, Beatrice clearly has a mind of her own and intends to resist any attempts to influence either her behaviour or her judgement. But by contrast, Hero's affections are rather more obviously subject to her father's control. The two alternative viewpoints are emphasised dramatically in the contrast between the 'advice' which Leonato has already given to his daughter concerning the advances which Don Pedro will make to her, and the more practical, down-to-earth, but frivolously expressed advice that Beatrice now offers to Hero. As the revellers enter, Leonato and the others put on their masks in preparation for the dance which is to follow. The action now moves between a series of dialogues whose main function is to establish a number of comparisons and contrasts, all emphasising the extent to which disguises can be more or less discovered. The final dialogue, between Benedick and Beatrice, comes abruptly to an end as they follow the other revellers out to the dance, leaving only Don John, Borachio, and Claudio on stage together.

Don John, acting on the information given to him earlier by Borachio (I.3.), and taking full advantage of Claudio's disguise, reveals to him that Don Pedro intends to woo Hero for himself. Claudio's reaction is one of immediate despondency, and when Don John and Borachio leave him, he concludes in a formal soliloquy that the information is correct. As if to corroborate Don John's story, Benedick enters with the news that Don Pedro has been successful in wooing Hero, and Claudio leaves the stage in a fit of pique. In a much more prosaic soliloquy, which provides a contrast to the one we have just heard from Claudio, Benedick meditates upon Beatrice's earlier apparent failure to penetrate his disguise, and he lightheartedly resolves to be revenged upon her for slandering him. Don Pedro, Leonato, and Hero now return in an effort to find Claudio, but they are told that he has left, crestfallen at Don Pedro's betrayal of his friendship. The picture Benedick paints of him is that of the typically 'romantic' lover, suffering the pangs of rejection, and he then turns to accuse Don Pedro of causing this state of affairs. Don Pedro responds by revealing the true extent of his involvement with Hero, and turns the conversation to the topic of mutual slander in which Beatrice and Benedick have been engaged. Benedick responds with an indulgent defence of his attitude, but as Beatrice approaches with Claudio, he beats a hasty retreat. Beatrice attributes Claudio's downcast state of mind to his jealousy, but when Don Pedro reveals the truth, his attitude changes completely, and while she and Don Pedro engage in a light-hearted battle of wits, he and Hero are silently reconciled. When Beatrice leaves, Leonato and Don Pedro discuss her suitability as a wife for Benedick, and they enlist the help of the newly reunited Claudio and Hero in bringing the two combatants together in marriage.

NOTES AND GLOSSARY

tartly:	sourly
heart-burned:	heartburn caused by the sour look on Don John's face
my . . . son:	a pampered child
tattling:	chattering
good . . . foot:	sound in body and limb
if 'a:	if he
good will:	consent
By . . . troth:	In truth (an oath)
shrewd:	sharp
too curst:	too savage
God's sending:	my natural attributes (that is, those that God has sent me)
that way:	in that direction
God . . . horns:	to the cow that is savage, God sends short horns to prevent her from doing too much damage
no horns:	a quibble upon 'husband' (Benedick had suggested earlier that all husbands wore cuckold's horns)
Just:	just so

at him:	praying to him
lie . . . woollen:	sleep between woollen blankets without sheets (hence in severe discomfort)
hath . . . beard:	a youth
apparel:	clothes
even . . . bearward:	a woman who died unmarried, and who, therefore, could lead no children to heaven, was thought to lead apes into hell. Also the 'bearward' or bear-keeper, who kept bears for baiting, kept apes. Beatrice is saying that she would be happy to take money from the bear-keeper for doing his job
cuckold:	a husband whose wife has been unfaithful to him
Saint Peter:	the keeper of the gates of heaven
for . . . heavens:	by heaven (an oath)
faith:	in faith (an oath)
make curtsy:	acknowledge the authority of her father
for . . . that:	in spite of all that
fitted:	provided
metal:	substance (but also 'spirit')
overmastered:	subjected to the authority of
clod . . . marl:	a piece of earth (Beatrice is alluding to the fact that Eve was made from Adam's rib and not from earth)
match . . . kindred:	marry my close relatives
solicit . . . kind:	propose to you
important:	importunate
Scotch-jig:	a lively dance
measure:	a more stately dance
cinquepace:	a lively dance based on five separate dance-steps
fantastical:	fanciful
ancientry:	custom and formality
bad legs:	physical infirmities
sink:	a pun on 'cinquepace', usually pronounced 'sink-pace'
apprehend:	understand (also 'anticipate')
passing:	very
good eye:	sound judgement
by daylight:	in realistic terms (seeing clearly and not being prepared to be duped by 'romantic' notions)
revellers:	dancers
a bout:	a turn (in partnership for the dance)
favour:	face (an ironic reference to Don Pedro's disguise)
God defend:	God forbid
lute . . . case:	the instrument (the 'inner' man) should be like the case (its outward appearance)

visor:	mask
Philemon's roof:	rough (Philemon was a peasant who entertained Jupiter in disguise, and the roof of his cottage was made of thatch)
Jove:	Jupiter, the senior God in the Roman pantheon
I would:	I wish
match me:	pair me
clerk:	parish official
waggling:	wagging or shaking
counterfeit:	imitate
ill-well:	with so successful an imitation of his deficiencies
dry . . . down:	completely shrivelled hand
Go to, mum:	Away with you and be silent (an expletive)
graces:	qualities
appear:	reveal themselves
there's . . . end:	that's the end of it
good wit:	sharp mind
'Hundred Merry Tales:	a popular book of jokes and stories
only his:	his only
libertines:	wastrels
commendation:	what recommends it
the fleet:	the company of dancers (a nautical metaphor)
boarded:	accosted (a rather ambiguous remark from Beatrice)
break . . . comparison:	make a satirical remark
peradventure:	perhaps
marked:	noted
partridge wing:	a small morsel (since the partridge wing has no meat on it)
leaders:	the leading dancers
turning:	turn in the dance (but also perhaps piece of fickle behaviour)
amorous on:	attracted to
break with:	tell
visor:	masked dancer
bearing:	deportment
equal . . . birth:	social equal
do:	perform
Save:	Except
blood:	passion
accident . . . proof:	a commonly proved occurrence
mistrusted not:	did not suspect
willow:	a tree associated with the passions of unreciprocated love

County:	Count
fashion:	style
garland:	adornment
usurer's chain:	a chain worn around the neck by successful merchants
lieutenant's scarf:	lieutenant's sash
one way:	one way or the other
drovier:	cattle-drover
so:	that is how
sedges:	undergrowth
puts . . . person:	places her own perverse meaning on things
gives . . . out:	lets it be known that I am
Lady Fame:	Rumour (usually personified as a woman)
lodge . . . warren:	a game-keeper's hut (a lonely place)
rod:	whip
flat transgression:	straightforward misdeed
not . . . amiss:	not in vain
your saying:	what you have just said
hath . . . you:	is angry with you
thaw:	melting of snow, which prevents people from going out and enjoying themselves
conveyance:	skill
mark:	target
poniards:	daggers
terminations:	expressions
infect:	spread disease to
Adam . . . transgressed:	all the virtues of Paradise before Adam fell from grace
Hercules . . . too:	an allusion to Omphale, who in Greek legend enslaved Hercules, making him dress in women's clothes (literally, make Hercules do the cooking, and break up his club for firewood)
infernal Ate:	goddess of mischief
apparel:	clothes
conjure:	influence her by magic
sanctuary:	a place of protection
perturbation:	cause of disturbance
command . . . service:	instruct me to perform any task
slightest:	most trivial
Antipodes:	the opposite side of the earth
toothpicker . . . Asia:	one who makes jewelled toothpicks (Asia was traditionally associated with elegant trinkets)
Prester . . . foot:	the foot of a legendary wealthy Christian king who lived in a remote part of Asia

great . . . beard:	the Emperor of China's beard
embassage:	errand
Pigmies:	legendary race of dwarfs reputed to live in North Africa
harpy:	monster
My . . . Tongue:	Beatrice is characterised by her tongue
false dice:	trickery
put . . . down:	demoralised
not . . . me:	just so long as he doesn't 'put me down' (steal my virginity and make me pregnant)
civil:	coldly courteous (but with a pun on 'Seville', a place in Spain famous for its oranges. Yellow was also the colour (complexion) of jealousy
blazon:	description of his face (literally, 'his coat-of-arms')
conceit:	view of what happened
cue:	opportunity
perfectest:	most perfect
little:	hardly
dote:	infatuated with
windy . . . care:	avoid being beset by worries
to . . . world:	gets married
sunburnt:	neglected because I lack elegance (literally because my skin is not delicate)
getting:	begetting
come by:	find or discover
matter:	seriousness
out . . . question:	unquestionably
star danced:	an astrological explanation of Beatrice's carefree attitude
cry . . . mercy:	beg your pardon
hear tell:	be told about (or simply 'to hear')
out . . . suit:	out of their courtship of her
were:	would be
go . . . church:	perform the wedding ceremony
goes . . . crutches:	goes slowly
rites:	solemn ceremonies
seven-night:	week
answer . . . mind:	all the questions that I want to ask answered
shake . . . head:	nod your head
breathing:	delay
warrant:	promise
interim:	meantime
Hercules' labours:	one of the twelve labours of Hercules the legendary Greek hero (a formidable task)

mountain . . . affection:	considerable affection
I . . . fain:	I would be glad to
have . . . match:	have the marriage arranged
fashion:	arrange
minister:	offer
as . . . direction:	according to my instructions
I . . . you:	I am the very person to help you
unhopefullest:	least hopeful
strain:	nature
humour:	make amenable
queasy:	squeamish
drift:	the direction of my thoughts

Act II Scene 2

Don John and Borachio now meet to discuss the failure of their first attempt to disrupt the proposed marriage between Claudio and Hero. But Borachio has another plan, far more dishonest than the first. He proposes to persuade Margaret, Hero's maid, to disguise herself in her mistress's clothes, and to act out a brief scenario with him in the presence of Claudio and Don Pedro. The disguising of the previous scene now takes on a rather more sinister tone as Borachio proposes to engineer an exchange of identities which will provide 'proof' of Hero's infidelity. He suggests that the plan be put into operation on the evening before the marriage is due to take place, and he urges Don John to persuade Claudio and Don Pedro to be present to witness the scenario. Both leave determined to play their respective parts in this villainous plot.

NOTES AND GLOSSARY

cross:	prevent
bar:	impediment
cross:	preventive measure
medicinable:	health-giving
athwart:	across
ranges . . . mine:	satisfies me
covertly:	secretly
since:	ago
in . . . favour:	am entertained by
unseasonable:	inappropriate
appoint her:	arrange with her that she
what life:	what potential
temper:	fashion or manufacture
spare not:	do not refrain from

marrying:	aiding the marriage of
do . . . up:	you must forcefully uphold
contaminated stale:	diseased prostitute
misuse:	abuse
issue:	conclusion
despite:	spite
meet:	appropriate
zeal:	earnestness
cozened:	duped
semblance:	appearance
instances:	examples
likelihood:	plausibility
fashion . . . matter:	arrange things

Act II Scene 3

The tone now lightens again with Don Pedro's plot to bring Benedick and Beatrice together in marriage. We are allowed a final glimpse of Benedick before his fall as he muses at the folly of Claudio in wanting to get married. He asserts in soliloquy that he does not think that he will ever become the kind of 'romantic' lover that his friend is, but at this point he sees Don Pedro, Claudio and Leonato approaching, and so he hides. Their pretext for being in Leonato's orchard is to hear Balthazar's music, but they have spotted Benedick in hiding, and plan to engineer a conversation which will give him the impression that Beatrice is in love with him. Benedick is to be made to think that he is overhearing a confidential conversation, and this will have the effect of convincing him more completely. From his hiding-place Benedick offers a few critical comments on the music, but he overlooks completely the significance of the song itself, which is about deception and inconstancy. Benedick remains privately critical, not suspecting any ulterior motive, while Balthazar is asked to play outside Hero's chamber-window on the following evening. There is just a hint here that Claudio himself will shortly be caught in his own trap.

When Balthazar leaves, Don Pedro turns to the question of Beatrice's apparent love for Benedick. Claudio and Leonato assist in the deception, while Benedick registers the full effect of their comments in a series of asides. He learns that Beatrice will never make her love known to him for fear of being ridiculed, although she apparently writes Benedick's name continually in a manner which, perhaps, has more in common with the 'romantic' relationship of Claudio and Hero than with her own more 'realistic' approach to human affairs. They pretend to fear how Benedick might ridicule her if he discovers her affection for him, and although they make some concessions to his character, they hint strongly that he should examine his own personality and attitudes with a view to becoming less scornful. They leave, believing that Benedick is completely hooked, and intending to lay the same trap for Beatrice.

When they have gone, a rather different Benedick emerges from his hiding-place. He tries to justify this change, but manages only a clever and earthy pretext for doing so, as Beatrice enters. He now regards her in a different, much more sympathetic light, even though we know that she has not yet fallen victim to the deceptions of Don Pedro and the others. Consequently, Benedick misinterprets all of her rather hostile remarks as signs of affection and at the end of the dialogue he is left alone on stage attempting to fit what she has said into the picture provided for him by Don Pedro and his accomplices.

NOTES AND GLOSSARY

hither:	here
am . . . already:	will do it very quickly
I . . . that:	Benedick responds by taking what his Boy has said literally
dedicates . . . behaviours:	devotes himself
argument . . . scorn:	the examples of the very thing he ridicules
fife:	small flute
tabor:	drum
afoot:	on foot
a . . . armour:	a suit of armour (possibly also 'an armoury of weapons')
carving . . . fashion:	designing the style
doublet:	waistcoat
was . . . to:	was inclined to
turned orthography:	become loquacious but pedantically so (lovers usually expressed their love in poetry of a rather ornate style, and Claudio is being described as being the very epitome of print itself)
just so:	of so many
see . . . eyes:	and still retain my present attitude
will . . . sworn:	will not swear
take . . . oath:	swear
come . . . grace:	be the beneficiary of my affections
never cheapen:	make an offer of marriage to her
angel:	a coin
arbour:	orchard
grace:	embellish
fit:	provide
hid-fox . . . pennyworth:	requite his cunning
tax not:	do not ask

put . . . perfection:	to be modest
woo:	persuade
suit:	courtship
yet:	even so
notes:	musical notes (Balthazar explores the alternative meaning 'noticing' in his reply)
crotchets:	musical notes of a particular kind, but also 'whims'
forsooth:	indeed
nothing:	possibly a pun on 'noting' since the two words are thought to have been pronounced in the same way
sheep's guts:	the gut strings of Balthazar's instrument, possibly a lute
hale:	drag
horn:	hunting horn, or military trumpet
for . . . money:	I prefer
blithe:	lighthearted
bonny:	merry
ditties:	verses
dumps:	sad songs
fraud . . . men:	the deception of men
leavy:	rich in leaves
for . . . shift:	as a makeshift
An:	If
bode:	foretell
had . . . lief:	would prefer to
night-raven:	a bird of ill-omen
plague:	catastrophe
stalk on:	hunt on
fowl:	bird (that is Benedick)
Sits . . . corner?:	Is that the way the wind is blowing?
counterfeit:	pretend
discovers it:	reveals it
gull me:	to dupe or trick me
knavery:	villainy
sure:	surely
ta'en infection:	caught the disease
hold . . . up:	keep it up
smock:	night-dress
writ:	written upon
pretty jest:	congenial joke
between . . . sheet:	between the sheet of paper (but also 'between the sheets in bed')
halfpence:	pieces (a halfpenny was a small coin)

railed at:	scolded
flout:	disdain
overborne:	overtaken
afeard:	afraid
some other:	someone else
discover:	reveal
an alms:	an act of charity
out . . . suspicion:	beyond any doubt
exceeding:	very
ten proofs . . . one:	it is ten to one that (that is, 'it is almost certain that')
blood:	passion
dotage:	infatuation
daffed:	laid aside
respects:	considerations
bate:	abate
proper:	respectable
in . . . mind:	in my view
by . . . jests:	to judge by some of the extravagant jokes
wear . . . out:	exhaust it
counsel:	advice
so good:	of so good
matter:	substance
dumb-show:	a scene in which there are actions but no words
sadly borne:	solemnly conducted
full bent:	full scope
detractions:	deficiencies
put . . . mending:	correct them
quirks:	clever remarks
railed:	ranted on
paper bullets:	harmless missiles
awe:	frighten
career . . . humour:	following his own inclinations
peopled:	populated
marks:	signs
daw withal:	fool with
Jew:	unchristian, and hence uncharitable

Act III Scene 1

With Benedick's behaviour towards Beatrice already transformed, attention is turned towards Beatrice herself, as Hero, Ursula, and Margaret prepare the trap for her. The verse dialogue of this scene presents a stark contrast to the lively and varied prose associated with the more realistic utterances of Benedick and Beatrice, and reinforces Hero's position as spokeswoman for the 'romantic' point of view in the play. Beatrice enters furtively, and hides while Hero and Ursula launch into their carefully prepared dialogue. She hears that Benedick is in love with her, but that her scornful and selfish attitude prevents anyone from telling her so. Her faults are emphasised, although Ursula pretends not to believe that Beatrice is so totally lacking in either judgement or compassion as to want to allow Benedick to suffer the pangs of unrequited love. They leave, confident that Beatrice is thoroughly convinced, and indeed, she emerges from hiding, a changed character. She no longer hates Benedick, nor is so contemptuous as she was, of marriage; her view is now more positive, and sympathetic, much less self-regarding even than that of her 'lover' in the previous scene.

NOTES AND GLOSSARY

parlour:	sitting-room
Proposing:	discussing
Whisper . . . ear:	Whisper in her ear
discourse:	conversation
pleached bower:	enclosure fenced with bushes (probably the same place where Benedick was gulled in the previous scene)
honeysuckles:	flowers of red clover
our propose:	discussion
Bear . . . well:	Do what you are supposed to do properly
trace . . . alley:	walk up and down this path
merit:	deserve
Cupid's crafty arrow:	the God of Love's skilfully made arrow (Hero refers here to the effect which their discussion will have on Beatrice)
lapwing:	plover
close by:	close to
golden oars:	fins
treacherous:	traitorous (the bait designed to betray her into captivity)
angle:	fish
couched:	crouched down
woodbine converture:	woodbine covering
coy:	disdainful
haggards:	wild female hawks
new-trothed:	newly betrothed
entreat:	beg
as full . . . upon:	as good a wife as Beatrice
framed:	fashioned

Misprizing:	Undervaluing
take . . . project:	conceive of any kind
self-endeared:	self-centred
sport:	a game
how . . . featured:	however handsome
spell . . . backward:	invert his qualities
antic:	an ugly fool
lance ill-headed:	a spear badly tipped
low:	short
agate:	a stone used in the carving of small figures
vilely:	badly
vane:	a weather-vane which shows the wind direction
carping:	demurring
from . . . fashions:	out of step with everyone
mock . . . air:	ridicule me into insignificance
counsel:	advise
honest:	not malicious
ill:	slanderous
empoison:	poison (used here in a metaphorical sense)
prized:	reputed
excepted:	with the exception
fancy:	imagination
shape:	looks
bearing:	posture
argument:	rationality
ere:	before
every day:	for ever
attires:	clothes
furnish:	provide
limed:	trapped
haps:	chance
fire . . . ears:	why are my ears burning so much (because someone is talking about Beatrice)
behind . . . such:	glory will not be gained from following the paths of 'contempt' and 'maiden pride'
holy band:	marriage
reportingly:	by what I have heard

Act III Scene 2

Don Pedro, Claudio, and Leonato now test Benedick to confirm that their plan to change his attitude towards Beatrice has been successful. Don Pedro reveals that after Claudio's wedding he intends to leave for Arragon, but he rejects Claudio's offer to accompany him, suggesting that he will have other, more pressing domestic commitments after his marriage. Instead he elects to be accompanied by the more misogynistic Benedick, who, he claims (with some conscious irony), remains hostile to women and love. Benedick tries to evade their questions, with Claudio continuing to harp on the fact that his friend must be in love, while Don Pedro comically seeks for an alternative explanation. Between them they manage to recast Benedick in the role of the very 'romantic' love that he has earlier sought to reject so vehemently. Benedick, realising that neither will grant him a sympathetic hearing, and afraid of being ridiculed, invites Leonato to join him in a private discussion.

They leave, and Claudio and Don Pedro review with some pleasure the success of their plan. But their victory is short-lived. Don John now approaches them with the startling news that Hero has been unfaithful, and that he can prove the allegation. The mood of the scene now changes to one of seriousness, as the plotters of Benedick's comic downfall are themselves the victims of a much more sinister plot. A shocked Claudio proclaims that if she has indeed been disloyal, then he will unmask her infidelity at the wedding ceremony itself. The scene ends with Don Pedro and Claudio lamenting this unforeseen change of fortune, and with Don John urging them to confirm the truth of his allegation by observing a 'sequel' which only we know he has prepared for them.

NOTES AND GLOSSARY

bring . . . thither:	accompany you there
vouchsafe me:	allow me
soil . . . gloss:	stain the newness
be bold:	presume to ask
cut . . . bowstring:	prevented Cupid from aiming his arrows of love
little hangman:	rogue
clapper:	hanging metal bar inside a bell
truant:	one who is unfaithful to his principles
wants:	needs
hang . . . draw:	hanging and drawing (disembowelling) were used in the execution of criminals
Where:	Where there
humour:	body fluid
fancy:	imagination
fancy:	penchant
slops:	loose trousers
'A:	He
o' mornings:	in the mornings
bode:	indicate
old . . . cheek:	his beard
stuffed tennis-balls:	used for stuffing the insides of tennis-balls

civet:	perfume
note:	sign
was . . . to:	was used to
paint:	use make-up
lute	the stringed instrument a lover used to accompany his songs
stops:	the frets on the fingerboard of the lute (but here there is a pun on 'stops' meaning 'hesitations')
tells:	indicates (but also 'weighs')
I warrant:	I'll bet
ill conditions:	unsavoury characteristics
dies:	will be prepared to go to bed with him
face upwards:	a bawdy reference to sexual intercourse
hobby-horses:	idiots
break . . . him:	broach the subject
by this:	according to this
bears:	the aggressive behaviour characteristic of bears
Good-e'en:	Good evening
if . . . served:	if it is convenient
I . . . that:	I don't know about that
discover:	reveal
aim . . . me:	arrive at a better understanding of my character
holds . . . well:	has a high regard for you
holp:	helped
effect:	put into effect
suit . . . spent:	effort wasted
ill bestowed:	misused
circumstances shortened:	without more ado
for . . . of:	since I have not yet got to the point
paint out:	give substance to
warrant:	proof
congregation:	those assembled for the church ceremony
disparage:	slander
bear . . . coldly:	control your anger
issue:	result
untowardly:	perversely
sequel:	what follows

Act III Scene 3

After the startling revelations of Don John, resulting in Claudio's formulation of a plan to disgrace Hero publicly if he finds her guilty of infidelity, the focus of attention moves to a group of minor characters, Dogberry, Verges, and the Watch, who are charged with preserving law and order in Messina. Ironically, this group of characters will exercise a decisive influence on the play's action, and on the resolution of the plot, although our first impressions suggest that such a role for them would be unlikely. The rather pompous Dogberry is presiding over the selection of a suitable constable, but the hilariously confused dialogue illustrates just how incompetent he and his fellows really are. Indeed, none of them seems to have a clear grasp of how language works, since they all, without exception, use words to express the exact opposite of what they intend. Having 'explained' very unclearly the duties of the Watch, and having elected a constable, Dogberry and Verges leave, but as they depart they urge their colleagues to pay special attention to Leonato's house, since it will be the focal point of the wedding preparations.

Almost as soon as Dogberry and Verges have gone, Conrade and Borachio appear and they engage in a conversation which the Watch fortuitously overhears. The two villains discuss the arranged incident devised to prove Hero's guilt, and we learn that the first part of Don John's plan has already been accomplished. Ominous though this sounds, the full seriousness of the threat is alleviated since almost before the plan has been fully completed the villainy has been discovered, and by the most unlikely means imaginable. The Watch may not be particularly adept at expressing themselves, as the apprehension of Conrade and Borachio shows, but they can recognise villainy when they see it, and proceed to arrest the two after their own comical fashion. The arrest of Conrade and Borachio introduces an element of suspense into the action since the question arises whether the discovery of the full implications of their plot can be made before Claudio's public disgrace of Hero.

NOTES AND GLOSSARY

Yea:	Yes
salvation:	Dogberry really means 'damnation'
Nay:	No
allegiance:	loyalty
charge:	duties
desartless:	Dogberry really means 'deserving'
hither:	here
well-favoured:	handsome
gift . . . fortune:	an accident of fortune
come . . . nature:	is natural (perhaps with an unintended pun on 'natural' meaning 'fool')
which:	of which
favour:	looks
senseless:	Dogberry really means 'sensible'

constable:	an officer whose job it is to enforce the law
bear:	carry
lantern:	light
charge:	duty
comprehend:	Dogberry means 'apprehend'
vagrom men:	vagabonds
stand:	halt
knave:	villain
bidden:	ordered to
none:	not one
meddle:	interfere
babble:	prattle
tolerable:	Dogberry means 'intolerable'
what belongs:	what are the duties
ancient:	old
should offend:	should be offensive
bills:	spears with axeheads (similar to halberds)
make . . . not:	do not give you
by . . . office:	because you are the Watch
true:	honest
meddle . . . make:	meddle or have anything to do with them
the more is:	the better is
lay hands:	arrest
pitch:	tar (a reference to the biblical proverb 'He that toucheth pitch shall be defiled therewith', in the Apocryphal book of Ecclesiasticus 13:1)
take:	apprehend
by . . . will:	wilfully
ewe . . . bleats:	a proverbial saying
charge:	orders
present:	represent
stay:	apprehend
by'r Lady:	by our Lady, the Virgin Mary, (an oath)
'a:	he
Five . . . on't:	I'll bet you five to one
statutes:	laws
marry:	indeed
an:	if
chances:	happens
keep . . . counsels:	be discreet
coil:	noise or disturbance
vigitant:	Dogberry means 'vigilant'
Mass:	By the Mass (an oath)
scab:	sore

owe ... answer:	requite you
close:	secretly
pent-house:	overhanging roof
dear:	expensive
make ... price:	ask what fee
unconfirmed:	inexperienced
fashion:	Borachio takes up the question of ephemerality associated in the opening scene of the play with Benedick and with inconstancy generally
doublet:	waistcoat
nothing ... man:	is not part of a man's inner substance (this refers to the distinction between 'appearance' and 'reality', upon which Don John's plot depends)
apparel:	dress
Deformed:	the Watch thinks that the thief's name is 'Deformed' (and in a curious way he is correct since Don John's plot is based on an aberration of the truth)
this ... year:	for the past seven years
vane:	weather-vane, usually found on a church steeple, and used for telling the direction of the wind
giddily:	confused
hot-bloods:	eager or lusty men
Pharaoh's soldiers:	the soldiers of the king of Egypt who were drowned pursuing Moses and the Children of Israel across the Red Sea (a biblical story; see Exodus 14:28)
reechy painting:	dirty painting
god Bel's:	refers to the Babylonian god Bel and the Dragon destroyed by David. See the Apocryphal book of the Bible.
church window:	stained glass window (to be seen in a church)
Hercules:	a confusion with the biblical story of Samson whose hair was cut in order to deprive him of his strength (Judges 16:19)
smirched ... tapestry:	soiled and disintegrating picture
cod-piece:	a pouch worn by men which covered the abdomen
massy:	huge
club:	Hercules's weapon
wears ... apparel:	is far more changeable
giddy:	confused
shifted ... tale:	digressed from your story
wooed:	courted
by ... Hero:	calling her by Hero's name
she ... out:	she leans out
vilely:	badly

saw . . . off:	saw from a distance
possessed:	convinced
as . . . appointed:	as it had been arranged
o'er night:	during the night
recovered:	the Watch means 'discovered'
lechery:	the Watch means 'treachery'
commonwealth:	community
a' . . . lock:	he has a curl in his hair
made bring:	made to bring
obey:	the Watch means 'order'
like:	likely
goodly commodity:	valuable goods (meant ironically)
taken up:	arrested
bills:	the weapons carried by the Watch
commodity . . . question:	questionable merchandise

Act III Scene 4

It is now morning, and an unsuspecting Hero is preparing for her wedding. She discusses with Margaret (her servant who had impersonated her the previous night) what clothes she should wear for the ceremony, and they talk about 'fashion'. This concern with 'appearances' echoes the discussion in the previous scene between Conrade and Borachio, and reinforces the distinction between the 'appearance' of Hero's wedding, and the stark 'reality' which will turn out to be no wedding at all. Margaret is kept ignorant of the reason why she was asked to impersonate Hero, and in this scene her frankness is used to provide a striking dramatic contrast to the rather coy utterances of her mistress. Beatrice now enters, having been woken up, and in the dialogue with Margaret that follows, Beatrice's 'romantic' commitment to love contrasts vividly with the servant's critically detached point of view. In her frank speaking Margaret comes a little too close to the source of Beatrice's malady, and when she suggests an appropriate cure, the latter snaps back at her. But unlike the earlier Beatrice, whose preoccupation was with words alone, Margaret speaks nothing but the truth. The scene ends with Hero being 'dressed' for her wedding, although we know that, thanks to Don John, it is a wedding that will not take place.

NOTES AND GLOSSARY

rise:	get up
Troth:	In truth (an oath)
rebato:	a stiff collar
pray thee:	I beg you

Meg:	shortened form of Margaret
's not:	is it not
tire:	head dress
thought:	shade
rare fashion:	exquisite style (referring also to the 'fashion' of the previous scene)
exceeds:	is far superior to the praise it attracts
cloth . . . cuts:	woven gold material with slits revealing material of a contrasting colour
downsleeves:	close-fitting sleeves
side-sleeves:	long sleeves
underborne:	with a lining
tinsel:	silver and gold cloth
quaint:	dainty
weight . . . man:	a bawdy reference to the consummation of Hero's wedding
Fie . . . thee!:	Away with you!
Art not:	Are you not
honourably:	straightforwardly
an:	if
wrest:	distort
light:	trivial
heavy:	serious (but referring to Margaret's earlier bawdy reference to the 'weight of a man')
else:	otherwise
coz:	cousin
tune:	frame of mind, or temperament
Clap's:	Lead us into
'Light o' love':	the title of a popular song
burden:	bass (and hence male) accompaniment
light o'love:	make light of love (meaning also 'unchaste')
barnes:	barns (but with a pun on 'bairns' meaning 'babies')
construction:	interpretation
exceeding:	very
turned Turk:	changed your mind
sailing . . . star:	guiding oneself by familiar signs (sailors relied upon the north star for purposes of navigation)
trow:	I wonder
excellent perfume:	smell exquisitely
I . . . stuffed:	my nose is blocked (that is 'I have a cold')
stuffed:	lost your virginity (and possibly 'pregnant')
goodly:	splendid (but meant ironically)
professed apprehension:	become a knowledgeable person in the ways of the world (hence, possibly, 'cynical')

wear . . . cap:	display it (but Beatrice refers here also to the fool's cap, which was the sign of his folly)
Carduus Benedictus:	the thistle
qualm:	sickness
moral:	meaning
perchance:	perhaps
what . . . list:	what I want
such another:	something other than human
eats . . . grudging:	indulges himself without complaining
pace:	speed
false gallop:	Margaret is asserting that she speaks the truth (she uses an equestrian metaphor)

Act III Scene 5

While Hero is preparing herself for the wedding ceremony, Dogberry, Verges, and the Watch report their capture of Conrade and Borachio to Leonato. But Leonato is so busy that he does not have time to listen to the tedious digressions, or the petty rivalry between Dogberry and Verges. They are totally ignorant of the importance of the information they possess, and Leonato is irritated by their apparent inability to report it quickly and clearly. The tension is further increased when Leonato is called away on business, and when he orders that Dogberry himself must undertake the examination of Conrade and Borachio.

NOTES AND GLOSSARY

would you:	do you want
confidence:	Dogberry means 'conference' or 'conversation'
decerns:	Dogberry means 'concerns' (there is added irony here since the matter concerns Leonato very 'nearly' indeed)
Goodman:	used to refer to someone below the level of 'gentleman'
off . . . matter:	off the point
blunt:	Dogberry means 'sharp'
skin . . . brows:	proverbial saying, referring to the notion that honesty was to be seen in a man's face
odorous:	Dogberry means 'odious'
palabras:	speak briefly
for . . . part:	as far as I am concerned
tedious:	Dogberry mistakes the meaning of 'tedious'. He thinks it means 'rich'.
of:	upon
an't 'twere:	even if it were

exclamation:	Dogberry intends to compliment Leonato, but the word he uses means 'complaint'
I ... fain:	I would like to
excepting ... presence:	with your worship's permission
ha' ta'en:	have arrested
arrant knaves:	utter rogues
will be:	will persist in
it ... see!:	what a world we live in!
God ... man:	God is good (proverbial saying)
of:	on
broke bread:	ate food (hence 'lived')
comes ... you:	is smaller than you are
Gifts ... gives:	Dogberry misunderstands, thinking that Leonato is referring to his qualities, not his physical stature
comprehended:	Dogberry means 'apprehended'
aspicious:	Dogberry means 'suspicious'
suffigance:	Dogberry means 'sufficient'
ere:	before
stay ... you:	await you
inkhorn:	ink-well
examination:	Dogberry means 'examine'
none-com:	mad
set down:	record
excommunication:	Dogberry probably means 'examination'

Act IV Scene 1

Claudio, Hero, and the wedding party are now at the church. Leonato's fatherly nervousness, which reveals itself in his wish to have the ceremony concluded speedily, contributes to the generally tense atmosphere at the opening of the scene, but when Claudio gives Hero back to him in a cruel reversal of the wedding ceremony, he is shocked beyond belief. Claudio interprets all of Hero's reactions to his rejection of her as 'signs' of her guilt, and he even manages to persuade Leonato to adopt a similar view. Hero, of course, denies ever having been unfaithful but when the respectable Don Pedro interferes, and is further supported by his Bastard brother, a public picture is established of her as a thoroughly disreputable woman. Leonato despairs, Hero faints and is thought for the moment to have been struck dead, while Don John, Claudio, and Don Pedro storm out of the church leaving the congregation in disarray and confusion.

Of all those close to Hero, only Benedick and Beatrice show some direct concern for her well-being. Leonato, convinced for the moment that Claudio's interpretation of Hero's outward responses is accurate, disowns her in a speech full of self-pity. It is left to Beatrice to defend her cousin's honour, but she soon finds an ally in Friar Francis whose own interpretation of Hero's reactions during the ceremony is at odds with that of her accusers. When Hero revives and is questioned, she continues to assert her innocence; but the formality of the scene (it is in verse and not prose) coupled with Benedick's stumbling unawares upon the possibility that this mischief stems from Don John's malice, serve to prevent us from having our sympathies too fully engaged. Moreover, after an extravagantly indulgent outburst, Leonato now begins to soften a little towards Hero, and with the help of Friar Francis a plot is formulated to establish the truth or otherwise of Claudio's allegations. It is to be reported publicly that Hero died as a result of having been slandered, and that this will either bring Claudio to his senses, or, if she *is* guilty, allow Leonato to make discreet provision for her removal from public life altogether. Satisfied with Friar Francis's interim solution, all now leave, except Benedick and Beatrice who remain on stage together.

This is the first time that the couple have faced each other privately since the success of Don Pedro's plan to deceive them into believing that each is in love with the other, but their meeting at this crucial point in the play provides a vivid contrast to the separation of Claudio and Hero. Beatrice feels passionately that Hero is innocent, while Benedick admires the example of friendship which she provides. She still has some doubts about Benedick's ability to commit himself to any one course of action, but he responds with a direct and genuine declaration of love for her. Beatrice continues to be wary, but she finally relinquishes her evasiveness in a reciprocal declaration. Benedick responds with an extravagantly chivalric gesture in asking her to command him to do anything, but her reply is a surprisingly chilling one, and perhaps no less extravagant than the response of her lover: 'Kill Claudio'. Such a remark threatens the comic tone of the play, but the context in which it appears helps to modify our responses. Beatrice's command is couched in a dialogue which is, itself, predominantly lighthearted in tone, reminding us of the 'merry war' between the two characters earlier on in the play. Moreover, although Beatrice's command seems shocking to us, it is extravagant, and its force is quickly dissipated in a flurry of words with which she follows it up. It is only when the stuttering Benedick finally manages to ask her if she really believes that Hero has been wronged, in an exchange that is comic, that he accepts her command.

NOTES AND GLOSSARY

plain form: omitting the preamble to the wedding ceremony
recount: give a detailed account of
hither: here

inward impediment: secret obstacle
conjoined: joined together
charge: urge
Interjections?: Interruptions?
some: that is, some of the interruptions (Benedick makes light of what Claudio is saying)
Stand . . . by: stand aside
by . . . leave: with your permission
unconstrained: unforced
counterpoise: be of equal weight
render: give
again: back again
learn me: instruct me in
thankfulness: gratitude
semblance: appearance
authority: validity
cunning: clever (but underhanded)
withal: with
blood: blush
witness: testify to
heat . . . bed: what it is to be promiscuous
guiltiness: guilt (Claudio offers here an alternative interpretation of Hero's outward behaviour. He interprets 'signs' in the light of previous knowledge, but that too is based on 'appearance')
knit: join
approved: confirmed
wanton: loose woman
Dear my lord: My dear lord
in . . . proof: in order to test her yourself
vanquished: overcome
made defeat: persuaded her to give up (Leonato's use of martial imagery here suggests that he thinks Claudio may have forced Hero to submit)
would say: am going to say
known: had sexual intercourse with
extenuate: pardon or excuse
'forehand: beforehand (Claudio is referring to the practice of a 'contract' marriage, common in Elizabethan times, which would allow Hero and himself to behave as though they were married. Their promise would be binding before the formal ceremony)
word . . . large: extravagant or immodest language
bashful: modest

comely:	fitting
seemed . . . ever:	did I ever appear
Out . . . thee:	Away with you
write . . . it:	denounce it
Dian . . . orb:	Diana was the Roman moon-goddess, patroness of chastity and hunting, but her name was often used as a personification of 'the moon'. Hence, the phrase means 'the moon in its orbit'
blood:	desires of the flesh
ere . . . blown:	before it has blossomed
intemperate:	uncontrolled
blood:	passion
Venus:	in classical mythology, Venus the Goddess of Love, committed adultery with Mars, the God of War, and was ensnared in a net with her lover by her husband Vulcan, the blacksmith of the Gods
pampered:	overfed
sensuality:	lust
wide:	loosely (bawdily)
gone about:	contrived
link:	bring together
stale:	prostitute
nuptial:	wedding
Stand I:	Do I stand
move . . . question:	ask one question of
bid:	command
charge:	order
as:	because
beset:	surrounded
catechizing:	questioning
just reproach:	fair criticism
Marry:	the Virgin Mary (an oath)
that . . . Hero:	Hero's name itself can do that
itself:	herself
yesternight:	last night
betwixt:	between
grieved:	suffering
liberal:	gross or licentious
vile encounters:	lewd meetings
without . . . them	to utter them without giving offence
much misgovernment:	excessive evil conduct
hadst thou:	would you have
outward graces:	apparent virtues
placed:	situated

about:	around or in
counsels . . . heart	emotions
impiety:	irreverence
impious:	irreverent (Claudio sees in Hero a series of contradictions which he registers in his use of the literary figure of speech: oxymoron, a joining together of contradictions)
conjecture:	suspicion
Wherefore:	Why
thus:	in this way
smother . . . up:	stifle her
cover:	disguise
printed . . . blood:	reveals itself in her blushes
ope:	open
did . . . think:	if I thought
Thought I:	if I thought
on . . . rearward:	immediately behind (that is, 'following')
reproaches:	disgraces
Grieved . . . one?:	Did I lament the fact that I only had one child?
Chid:	did I scold
frugal . . . frame:	thrifty Nature's plan
one . . . thee:	one too many as shown by your example
wast:	were
issue:	offspring
smirched:	stained
mired:	muddied
on:	of
Valuing . . . her:	in my estimation of her
pit . . . ink:	black (and hence 'evil') pit (suggesting 'Hell')
season:	relish
attired:	wrapped up (Benedick uses a metaphor of 'clothes' here, in keeping with the theme of appearances generally which the play explores)
belied:	maligned
bedfellow:	that is, 'Did you sleep with her?'
barred . . . iron:	supported by iron bars (in other words 'what was already strong is now made even stronger')
Hence . . . her:	get away from her
this . . . fortune:	let things go so far
By noting:	because I have been observing (the Friar's observation of her outward appearance now calls forth an alternative interpretation of Hero's behaviour)
apparitions:	shadows
start into:	appear suddenly

angel whiteness: white as the colour of angels, and hence pure

fire: fire was used to consume evil things (the metaphor is used here to suggest that Hero's innocence is as a fire which consumes the heretical view that Claudio holds of her)

experimental seal: the testimony of experience

warrant: give substance to

tenor: nature

book: Hero is described as a 'book' which the Friar claims, by experience, to be able to read (contrast this with Leonato's use of the metaphor of 'printing' earlier, and which suggests that he does not know how to 'read' his own daughter)

biting error: vicious mistake

perjury: lying on oath

not denies: does not deny

proper nakedness: openly

warrant: allows

lack: be without the possibility

conversed: spoke

unmeet: inappropriate

yesternight: last night

maintained . . . words: conversed with (exchanged words with)

misprision: misunderstanding

bent: fully inclined to

practice . . . lives: it is . . . who is the source of this calumny

toil: twists in torment

frame: formulating

eat: has eaten

invention: ingenuity

made . . . means: so ruined my faculties

bad life: evil living

refit: deprived

in . . . kind: in such a way

policy . . . mind: mental strategy

ability . . . means: the means to carry out my plans

quit . . . them: to allow me to deal with them

sway: persuade

mourning ostentation: an outward show of grief

monument: gravestone

rites: rituals

appertain: that are appropriate to

well carried: well executed

travail: work

maintained:	argued
so . . . out:	it is always the case
prize . . . worth:	we do not estimate its full value
Whiles:	While
lacked . . . lost:	deprived of it and having lost it
rack:	extend to its extreme
fare:	turn out to be the case
study . . . imagination:	thoughts
apparelled:	dressed
habit:	clothes
moving:	exciting
eye . . . prospect:	range of vision
interest . . . liver:	in classical times, and right up to the Elizabethan period, the liver was thought to be where the passions and love particularly were situated
fashion:	make
lay . . . down:	describe it
likelihood:	in theory
aim:	conjecture
levelled:	aimed
quench:	extinguish
sort . . . well:	does not reach the conclusion we are hoping for
reclusive:	secretive
inwardness:	inner feelings
deal:	proceed
this:	this matter
flow . . . grief:	since I am overcome with grief
twine:	piece of thread
Presently:	Immediately
strain:	make equally strange
even:	precise
office:	duty
sauce:	relish
eat it:	deny your promise
devised to:	thought of for
What offence:	For what misdemeanour
stayed:	given me support
happy hour:	fortunately
Tarry:	Stay
approved . . . height:	confirmed in the extreme
kinswoman:	relative
bear . . . hand:	lead her on (with the intention of deceiving her)
take hands:	join their hands in marriage
uncovered:	open

unmitigated rancour: uncontrolled hatred
out at: from out of
proper: fine (ironical)
counties: counts
count: charge (with a pun on Claudio's title)
Comfect: Sweetmeat
melted . . . curtsies: is reduced to manners
compliment: extravagant praise
tongue: words (compare Beatrice's allegation with that levelled against her earlier in the play: II.1. 'I cannot endure my Lady Tongue')
trim: pretty (ironical)
with wishing: by wishing to be one
that . . . lie: who only uses words (but who does not support them with actions)
engaged: committed
render . . . account: shall pay dearly for what he has done

Act IV Scene 2

The public disgrace of Hero is the point towards which the main action of the play has been moving, but with the Friar's plan to vindicate her innocence, the focus shifts to the antics of the Watch in an attempt to provide a light-hearted balance to the more serious aspects of the plot. Dogberry, Verges, and the Watch now undertake to examine Conrade and Borachio. Dogberry and his colleagues comically mangle words themselves as they continue to say the precise opposite of what they mean. Dogberry particularly, is very much concerned that the formalities of the court hearing be observed, although the Sexton points out to him that he is not going about the business of examining the prisoners correctly. Finally, and through a smoke-screen of confused language, Don John's plot is revealed. The court learns, however, that Don John himself has fled and that Hero has died after having been publicly humilated (exactly the plan that the Friar had formulated). The Sexton orders Conrade and Borachio to be taken to Leonato's house but they offer some resistance, calling Dogberry as 'ass' and a 'coxcomb', insults to his dignity which he feels unable to overlook. The scene ends with a very defensive Dogberry asserting his own integrity in the face of these insults, and with the prisoners being led off to Leonato's house.

NOTES AND GLOSSARY
dissembly: Dogberry means 'assembly'
malefactors: criminals (Dogberry clearly mistakes the meaning of the word, and applies it to the Watch)

exhibition:	the complaint which has been submitted (it also means 'gift' and it may well be that Verges here mistakes the meaning of the word)
sirrah?:	sir?
God defend:	God forbid (an oath)
knaves:	rogues
it ... near:	it will almost be
go ... with:	establish my superiority
'Fore God:	Before God
in ... tale:	in collusion
eftest:	easiest
perjury:	Dogberry means that the accused is a liar, but perjury means 'lying on oath' and in this context is directed wrongfully at the Watch
Pray thee:	I beg you
peace:	be quiet
heard you:	did you hear
else:	in addition
Marry:	the Virgin Mary (an oath)
ducats:	silver coins
burglary:	Dogberry again uses the wrong word
by mass:	by the mass (an oath)
upon ... words:	having taken Don John's word
redemption:	Dogberry means 'damnation', hence the accused would go to hell
stolen away:	departed
in ... manner:	in this way
bound:	bound over (held in custody, but also literally 'tied')
go before:	precede
opinioned:	Dogberry means 'tied', but he uses the wrong word
coxcomb:	fool
naughty varlet:	worthless rascal
suspect:	Dogberry means 'respect'
write ... down:	record that I am
piety:	Dogberry uses the wrong word again
upon:	against
good witness:	sound observation
householder:	one who owns a house (and therefore someone to be respected)
pretty ... flesh:	as handsome as
go to	away with you
rich ... enough:	prosperous enough man
losses:	Dogberry means that he is not as rich as he was
writ down:	recorded

Act V Scene 1

The final act of the play begins with Antonio trying to comfort Leonato, who continues to grieve for the plight of Hero. Leonato's irrationality is made to contrast with the detached and objective commonsense advice that his brother gives him, but he responds by refusing to accept Antonio's advice until he too has undergone a similar kind of suffering. While we may feel that Leonato is being rather self-indulgent, especially when we remember that Hero is not dead, there is also a sense in which Antonio is being too theoretical.There is something to be said for Leonato's identifying the kind of inconsistency which is part and parcel of being human, although Antonio is also right to point out that to indulge in irrational behaviour is childish. But, paradoxically, Antonio's rational arguments are shown to lead to irrational actions with his suggestion that Leonato should direct his energies outward towards Claudio and Don Pedro in an act of revenge. The possibility of a confrontation is accelerated with the entry of Claudio and Don Pedro, although Leonato's challenge to Claudio is couched in terms which make it rather difficult for us to determine exactly how serious it is meant to be. Obviously he feels deeply the insult of having his daughter publicly disgraced, but on the other hand, our sympathies are only partly engaged because we know that Hero is still alive, and that a plot is in hand to try to induce Claudio to change his mind. If this is the beginning of the attempt to test Claudio, then it would appear to be unsuccessful since both he and Don Pedro remain adamant that their cause is just. But the surprise comes when Antonio, who a moment earlier has been advising rational behaviour, now becomes totally irrational himself as he issues an extravagant challenge to Claudio. He accuses his adversary of being no more than a semblance of manhood, but this is to no avail since, despite Leonato's unsuccessful attempts to interfere, Don Pedro and Claudio remain steadfast in their conviction. Leonato leaves, asserting that his point of view should be heard, but in the passionate outburst of his brother he has had the opportunity to observe a mirror-image of his own irrationality. Although Claudio has survived this challenge, we fear a rather more serious confrontation as Benedick now enters. Benedick, formerly a dispassionate observer of human behaviour, is now passionately involved as a result of his love for Beatrice, so that while Claudio and Don Pedro make light of their recent encounter with Leonato and Antonio, he remains solemn and serious. Their attempts to try to persuade him to resume his characteristically witty posture fail, and he issues a private challenge to Claudio, who, for his part, persists in trying to laugh off the seriousness of the situation. Don Pedro manages to change the subject by reporting Beatrice's assessment of Benedick's inconstancy, and Claudio supports the efforts of his friend by hinting obliquely at the earlier plot to deceive both Benedick and Beatrice. This mocking of Benedick's inconsistency, reminding him of his earlier promises to remain a bachelor, and recalling the extent to which he has already been duped, help to alleviate some of the seriousness of his challenge so that even though he will not be diverted from his task, we are made clearly aware of the fact that he is, himself, being manipulated, and is no less inconsistent than all the other characters involved in this scene so far.

When Benedick has left, Claudio and Don Pedro discuss his curious behaviour suggesting (by the apt use of the now familiar metaphor of 'clothes') that his over-serious attitude argues some deficiency in him, and that his excessive passion has distorted an otherwise balanced outlook. Don Pedro, however, is now having second thoughts as a result of the information which Benedick has just given him concerning Don John's escape from Messina, but he has little time to ponder the consequences of his brother's action before Dogberry, Verges, the Watch and their two prisoners enter. Don Pedro's suspicions are confirmed when he sees the bound figures of Conrade and Borachio, and, after a hilarious but characteristically confusing account from Dogberry, Borachio reveals the details of Don John's plot. The news of Hero's innocence shocks Claudio into a pained silence, but it produces exactly the effect that the Friar had hoped news of Hero's death would have upon him. Leonato, Antonio, and the Sexton now enter, and in the face of Leonato's persistence in sustaining the pretence of bitterness, Claudio and Don Pedro accept responsibility for their misguided view of Hero. Leonato responds by initiating the final stage of the Friar's plot by offering to marry Claudio to his 'niece'. We guess, of course, that the 'niece' in question is none other than Hero herself. Claudio agrees to abide by this suggestion, and Leonato now turns to examining the culprits. Borachio speaks out, vindicating Margaret's innocence, but Dogberry insists that he be questioned about the matter of the insults he received when trying to arrest the two. Leonato dismisses the Watch kindly and with typically confused replies Dogberry and his colleagues leave. The scene ends with Claudio being reminded of his promise both to honour Hero's grave, and to present himself for marriage to Leonato's 'niece' the following morning.

NOTES AND GLOSSARY

thus: like this
second: support
counsel: advice
sieve: a container with holes in it used for sifting powdery substances
suit: accord

strain:	strand
lineament:	contour
sorry way:	pathetic fool
proverbs:	concentrated expressions of wisdom
candle-wasters:	those who spend their time reading and thinking (hence 'theoreticians')
preceptical medicine:	a cure consisting of rational arguments
Fetter:	Bind
office:	duty
speak:	speak of
wring:	suffer pain
advertisement:	advice
Therein:	In that
nothing differ:	are no different
flesh . . .blood:	passionate (and hence 'human')
writ . . .style:	written in the manner of the Gods
made . . .push:	disregarded
chance . . .sufferance:	fortune and suffering (Leonato seeks to distinguish between the stability and superiority of the writings of philosophers and human behaviour itself)
bend not:	do not direct
speak'st reason:	speak reasonably (ironically Antonio is being irrational since his advice to 'revenge', understandable though it may be, is advice to perform an irrational act)
belied:	maligned
hastily:	in haste
Good e'en:	Good evening
have . . .haste:	are in haste
all is one:	no matter
right:	do justice to
lie low:	be dead
dissembler:	deceiver
beshrew:	curse
meant nothing:	Claudio refutes the meaning of his gesture, which is clearly an aggressive one
fleer:	scoff
jest:	joke
dotard:	an old man in his dotage
under . . . age:	being allowed the privilege of speaking because I am old
to . . . head:	to your face (hence 'directly')
bruise . . . days:	notwithstanding the effects of a long life
trial . . . man:	personal combat

nice fence:	dexterity with a sword
active practice:	continual practising
May . . . youth:	youthfulness
bloom . . . lustihood:	blossoming of his strength
have . . . to:	have anything to do with
daff:	cast aside
Win . . . me:	overcome me and brag of your victory
whip:	beat
foining fence:	thrusting style of fencing
apes:	fools (but also 'imitators of manhood')
Jacks:	contemptible men
milksops!:	babies!
Hold . . . content:	Remain contented
weigh:	are worth
scambling:	argumentative
out-facing:	bold or brazen-faced
cog:	cheat
flout:	brag
anticly:	fantastically
speak off:	sound off
durst:	wanted to
deal in:	deal with
wake . . . patience:	crave your indulgence
smart:	hurt
part . . . fray:	stop a fight
had . . . to:	were likely to have had
high-proof melancholy:	extremely sad
would . . . have:	would be glad to have
scabbard:	sheath for a sword
Never . . . so:	Nobody ever did
beside:	Claudio puns on Don Pedro's 'by thy side'
minstrels:	musicians
draw:	to draw a bow across a stringed musical instrument
Pleasure:	please
What:	Come now,
mettle:	spirit
your . . . career:	your joviality in full flight
an:	if
charge:	level (as one might aim a weapon)
staff:	lance
broke cross:	broken in two
turn . . . girdle:	prepare himself to fight
God . . . from:	God save me from
make . . . good:	justify it

how ... dare:	in whichever way you wish
Do ... right:	Accept my challenge
so ... cheer:	provided I am given a good welcome
feast:	Don Pedro takes the alternative meaning thinking that Claudio is referring to a banquet
bed:	said
calf's ... capon:	signs of folly and weakness
curiously:	carefully
knife's naught:	my sword is not worth anything (Claudio continues the metaphor of feasting)
woodcock:	fool
ambles:	rides easily along
the tongues:	has knowledge of other languages
forswore:	retracted his oath
double-tongue:	a sign of duplicity
transhape:	transform
wast:	were
properest:	finest
God ... garden:	an oblique reference to Benedick's hiding in the orchard (II.3), but Claudio alludes also to Adam hiding in the Garden of Eden, after having eaten of the forbidden fruit on the tree of knowledge. Benedick has 'fallen' as a result of his passion for Beatrice just as Adam fell because of his love for Eve (Genesis 3)
savage ... horns:	refers to Benedick's earlier assertion that all husbands were cuckolds
gossip-like humour:	prattling attitude
break jests:	crack jokes
braggarts:	boasters
discontinue ... company:	break off my friendship with you
Lackbeard:	one who has no beard (hence 'boy')
in earnest:	serious
pretty:	fascinating (ironical)
doublet ... hose:	waistcoat and long stockings (but meaning 'undressed')
leaves ... wit:	does not put on his sense of humour
giant ... ape:	a formidable opponent to a fool
doctor:	a wise man
to:	by comparison with
soft you:	just a moment
pluck up:	rouse
ne'er:	never
looked to:	taken care of

weigh . . . balance:	Dogberry alludes to the personified figure of Justice, who, in classical tragedy, weighed the guilt or innocence of those brought before her.
Hearken after:	Listen to
secondarily:	secondly (Dogberry confuses the order of the charges against Conrade and Borachio)
lay . . . charge:	accuse them of doing
his . . . division:	according to the categories laid down by Dogberry
by . . . troth:	on my honour
suited:	appropriate
bound . . . answer:	held in custody to answer charges
cunning:	clever (meant ironically)
go . . . answer:	proceed no further in my own defence
incensed:	incited
seal:	confirm
Runs . . . iron:	Does not this speech pierce you like the blade of a sword?
while:	while
set . . . on:	urge you
practice:	execution
upon:	as a result of
rare semblance:	exquisite appearance
plaintiffs:	Dogberry means 'defendants'
reformed:	Dogberry means 'informed'
when . . . serve:	at the appropriate time
bethink . . . patience:	beg your forbearance
Impose . . . to:	Impose upon me
invention:	imagination
bend . . . weight:	buckle under any suffering
enjoin:	impose upon
Possess:	Inform
labour:	bring forth
embrace:	seize upon
henceforth:	for the future
naughty:	worthless
packed in:	an accomplice
by her:	done by her
not . . . black:	has not been recorded
plaintiff:	Dogberry means 'defendant'
beseech:	beg
Deformed:	like the Watch, Dogberry mistakes an adjective for a proper name
hard-hearted:	ungenerous
examine:	question

foundation:	charitable institution (Dogberry again uses the wrong form of address)
depart:	Dogberry uses the wrong grammatical construction here
prohibit:	Dogberry really means 'permit'
look . . . you:	will expect you
lewd:	worthless

Act V Scene 2

Attention now switches briefly to the Benedick-Beatrice plot, with Benedick seeking Margaret's help in trying to arrange an interview with Beatrice. For the moment Benedick takes upon himself the role of romantic lover, eager to attempt to write sonnets in praise of his mistress, but Margaret brings the conversation down to a more realistic and earthy level with her witty undermining of his attitude. Margaret goes off to find Beatrice leaving Benedick alone attempting to translate his love into poetic terms. After a number of unsuccessful attempts at rhyming he decides that the role of romantic lover is not for him, and reverts to his earlier directness, just as Beatrice herself enters. She immediately wants to know the outcome of his encounter with Claudio, but when she learns that all they did was to exchange 'words', she offers to leave. Benedick upbraids Beatrice for mistaking his meaning, and gives her a more detailed account of what passed between him and Claudio. He then changes the subject, directing his attention to Beatrice's love for him, and what follows is a dialogue full of ingenuity, but one which is without the hostility and venom of some of the earlier exchanges. Benedick now asks about Hero, and is optimistic about her recovery, but Ursula comes rushing in with the news that Don John's plot has been discovered. All three then leave in haste for Leonato's house, with Benedick accepting Beatrice's invitation to accompany her in a style which combines sexual realism with a parody of romantic excess.

NOTES AND GLOSSARY

deserve . . . hands:	give me the opportunity to reward you
the speech:	conversation with
high:	inflated
come . . . it:	write a better one
comely:	fitting
come . . . me:	be my husband
keep . . . stairs:	never rise to the status of mistress
catches:	secures its quarry
fencer's foils:	swords with the points capped

I . . . bucklers:	I submit to your superiority
bucklers:	shields
pikes:	spikes at the centre of a shield
vice:	screw (but this, along with the rest of the dialogue, contains a great deal of sexual innuendo)
Leander:	in classical legend Leander swam the Hellespont in order to be with his mistress Hero.
Troilus:	the lover of Cressida (he was considered an example of devotion, while she was a model of inconstancy). The story appeared originally in Homer's *Iliad*, translated in 1598 by George Chapman.
panders:	go-betweens
quondam carpet-mongers:	former frequenters of ladies' drawing-rooms
yet:	still
even road:	balanced passage
turned over:	harassed
innocent:	silly
festive terms:	formal language
ere:	before
with . . . came:	with what I came for
thereupon:	upon that
noisome:	obnoxious
frighted . . . word:	scared language
right:	correct
undergoes:	is under the burden of
subscribe him:	acknowledge him to be
maintained . . . evil:	comprised so well-organised a state of evil
intermingle:	mix
suffer:	Beatrice takes its alternative meaning of 'put up with'
instance:	example
that . . . neighbours:	current at the time when people did not quarrel
Question:	My reply to your question is as follows
clamour:	noise
quarter . . . rheum:	a quarter of an hour in tears
Don Worm:	the 'worm of conscience' which causes indecision in man's mind
impediment:	obstacle
trumpet:	sound of
bear witness:	testify
mend:	get better
old coil:	turmoil
presently:	immediately
die . . . lap:	a bawdy reference to sexual orgasm

Act V Scene 3

It is night, and in a solemn ceremony Claudio now undertakes to carry out the first part of his promise to Leonato, in his mourning of Hero's death. He speaks a formal epitaph over her grave, acknowledging that her reputation will live on even though she is (as he thinks) dead. After a solemn song, Claudio promises to perform these rites annually, and as morning breaks he and Don Pedro look forward to another, less solemn, ceremony. This scene is not without some irony since we know what Claudio and Don Pedro do not know, that Hero is still alive. Rather, just as in the case of Benedick's promise, Claudio is now being put to the test, and each strand of the plot is being drawn together in what will be a composite statement confirming the virtue of constancy.

NOTES AND GLOSSARY

monument:	grave
guerdon:	reward
goddess ... night:	Diana, the Goddess of Chastity
virgin knight:	Hero herself
moan:	lament
wheels ... Phoebus:	Phoebus the Sun-God in classical legend and hence the bringer of day, who rode in his chariot (Don Pedro is saying that it is now dawn)
Dapples:	covers with spots
drowsy east:	the east is pictured as being still drowsy when awakened by day itself
several:	separate
weeds:	clothes
Hymen:	the God of Marriage
speed's:	speed us on our way
issue:	conclusion
woe:	lament

Act V Scene 4

The final scene of the play draws together on stage the two parallel plots involving Claudio and Hero on the one hand, and Benedick and Beatrice on the other. In an episode which is distinctly reminiscent of the masque in Act II, Scene 1, Leonato and Hero prepare themselves to receive Claudio. The Friar's plot, along with Leonato's additions to it, to change Claudio's mind, has been successful, and some attempt is now made to stress that blame cannot be attached to either side. Moreover, Benedick, who is also present, is relieved that he will not now have to fight Claudio. The ladies withdraw in order to put on their masks, and Benedick approaches the Friar to ask if he will be prepared to extend the ceremony in order to perform a marriage between himself and Beatrice. In reminding us (and those characters on stage who have been party to the plot to bring Benedick and Beatrice together) of the deception which this has involved, Leonato once again brings to the fore the theme of deception which will shortly receive one further ramification in the conclusion of the plot to bring Claudio and Hero together. But Benedick, who is not yet party to the plot to deceive him, and unaware of how he has been manipulated, is not to be diverted with incomprehensible innuendoes. With the entry of Claudio and Don Pedro, we are reminded of the earlier ceremony of Act IV, Scene 1, except that now Claudio reiterates an intention to be constant to his promise to marry Leonato's 'niece'. While Antonio goes to fetch the masked Hero, Don Pedro and Claudio turn their attention to a brooding Benedick. They begin to ridicule him for violating the views he had expressed so vehemently against marriage in the opening scenes of the play. Benedick just manages a cutting retort to Claudio as Antonio returns with the masked ladies. He proceeds to give Hero to Claudio, but the latter is prepared to accept her even before he has had the opportunity of discovering who she is, so firm is his resolve.

When she finally reveals her identity the effect proves to be one of the rebirth of innocence, as Claudio's newly re-established faith in Hero's honour revives a reputation which was 'killed' by malicious slander. The Friar, who instigated the plot in the first place, offers to reveal the full details of his plan to Claudio after the ceremony so that all the participants will finally be in possession of the full knowledge which some of them have been denied throughout. With one marriage now confirmed, attention focuses on the Beatrice-Benedick union. Beatrice unmasks at Benedick's request, but, in addition to comparing notes with regard to the plot of which they have both been victims, they seem for a moment to revert to their earlier hostility to each other. But this is the first time that both have been called upon to reveal their affections publicly, and they seem to be protecting their inner feelings from too public a scrutiny. Even so, things have gone too far to fail now, and they drop the pretence when both Claudio and Hero produce written evidence of their love for each other. Finally, Beatrice and Benedick abandon 'words', which are capable of preventing mutual understanding, for a gesture of mutual affection (a kiss), affirming a new consistency of attitude which promises to withstand the good-natured jibing of Claudio.

The conclusion of this plot establishes the notion of 'man' as a creature of contradictions, who should not be treated too harshly for changing his mind in the light of experience. A formal dance is proposed to celebrate the two marriages, although Benedick is adamant that before any celebrations he intends to confirm his promise. Only when both plots have been concluded satisfactorily does a messenger enter with the news that Don John has been captured, but with the full exposure of evil, and with the measures already taken to combat it having proved successful, the punishment of the villain must not be allowed to interfere with the festivities.

NOTES AND GLOSSARY

debated:	discussed
true . . . question:	once the full details of the issue have been examined
sort:	have turned out
else:	otherwise
by . . . enforced:	forced by my oath
to . . . reckoning:	to pay
office:	role
confirmed countenance:	with a straight face (as though I meant it)
entreat . . . pains:	ask for your help
truth . . . is:	it is a fact that
eye . . . flavour:	looks favourably upon me
eye . . . lent:	Leonato refers to Hero's part in the plot to persuade Beatrice into thinking that Benedick loves her
requite:	return her affections
whereof:	of which (Leonato refers to his own part in the plot)
what's . . . will?:	what do you want?
is enigmatical:	has no clear meaning
for:	as for
my . . . will:	what I want to secure is your goodwill
stand . . . ours:	be of equal standing with your own
conjoined:	joined together
My . . . liking:	I wholly approve of your affections
And . . . help:	And I agree to help
here attend:	are waiting here for you
hold . . . mind:	am determined
Ethiope:	a black (and hence 'ugly') woman
February face:	wintry look
savage bull:	reminding Benedick of his earlier ridiculing of the state of marriage. The bull has horns, and horns were considered to grow in the forehead of a husband whose wife was unfaithful to him.
Tush:	away with you (an expletive)
tip . . . Europa:	tip your horns with gold as Jupiter did in classical legend when he changed his shape to a bull in order to carry off Europa
play:	imitate

amiable low:	affectionate bellow
leaped . . . cow:	seduced your mother
got:	fathered
calf:	referring to Claudio
feat:	exploit
Much . . . to:	similar to
bleat:	the sound made by a calf
For . . . you:	I will repay that remark
reckonings:	repayments
qualify:	explain
largely:	in full
presently:	immediately
Troth no:	Truly no
friendly recompense:	but as friends do
sworn upon't:	am certain of it
halting:	limping
pure:	simple
fashioned:	directed
hands . . . hearts:	this draws together the theme of the discrepancy between 'appearance' and 'reality'
for:	out of
great persuasion:	because of your persistence
consumption:	wasting away
stop . . . mouth:	shut you up
college:	school (or fraternity)
wit-crackers:	jokers
flout:	ridicule
humour:	bent of mind
epigram:	witty saying
beaten . . . brains:	overcome by wit
wear . . . him:	wear no fine clothes
purpose:	intend
giddy:	confused
beaten:	vanquished
in that:	since
unbruised:	unharmed
cudgelled:	clubbed
double-dealer:	liar
out . . . question:	without doubt
narrowly:	carefully
word:	promise
staff . . . reverend:	emblem of princely authority
horn:	an allusion to the horns of the cuckold
ta'en:	captured

Part 3

Commentary

Much Ado About Nothing is about 'misapprehensions, misprisions, misunderstandings, misinterpretations, and misapplications', to use A.P. Rossiter's phrase.* Each of the main characters in the play is the victim of deception, and it is because they are deceived that they act in the ways that they do. Although the central deception is directed against Claudio in an attempt to destroy his relationship with Hero, many critics have felt that it is the deceptions involving Beatrice and Benedick which provide the play's dramatic focus. Indeed, the wit combats of Benedick and Beatrice are far more attractive in theatrical terms than the rather more serious and formal business of the Claudio-Hero plot. Of the more recent criticisms of the play, that of Bertrand Evans is fairly typical; he tentatively suggests† that it is a 'structural fault that Beatrice and Benedick, resembling stars, but serving as planets outshine those about whom they revolve.'

This apparent juxtaposition of seriousness and lightheartedness raises significant questions about the overall tone of the play. For example, how closely does Shakespeare intend our sympathies to be engaged for the central characters themselves? Is Hero's plight a potentially tragic one, or is it simply part of a larger design which requires that considerable difficulties be placed in the paths of the lovers before a happy resolution can finally be reached? Moreover, does the action in which Claudio is involved (and which foreshadows the plight of Othello in the later tragedy) strike too serious a note in the otherwise comic atmosphere of the play, and is there any place for the kind of 'evil' that Don John represents in a comedy of this sort? These are just some of the questions which *Much Ado About Nothing* raises.

The title of the play suggests clearly that no matter how serious the various obstacles to happiness appear at first sight, they are, in the final analysis, exposed as being trivial. Don John's plot, sinister though it appears, is shown to be wholly without substance, but by contrast, in the case of Benedick and Beatrice, the insubstantiality of their early encounters gives way to a relationship which has all the signs of proving very substantial indeed. Thus, in the one plot 'something' (the allegations

*A.P. Rossiter, *Angel With Horns*, Longman, London, 1961, p.77.
†Bertrand Evans, *Shakespeare's Comedies*, Oxford University Press, Oxford, 1967, p.73.

made by Don John) is proved to be 'nothing', while in the other, 'something' (the relationship between Benedick and Beatrice) is actually made out of 'nothing'. Both plots are linked by the methods of deception used on the various characters involved, and both depend upon the process of observation for their effectiveness, along with all its attendant dangers. Indeed, it has been argued that the 'nothing' to which the play's title refers, is a pun on 'noting' (apparently the two words were pronounced the same by Elizabethans). Characters are made to 'note' or observe others, and are also made to misunderstand the significance of what they see and hear. Sometimes this misunderstanding has positive, and ultimately happy consequences, but at other times its dangers are emphasised. But the 'nothing' of the title may hint at yet another meaning, in that it may refer ironically to 'chastity'; in Marlowe's poem *Hero and Leander*, (from which Shakespeare seems to have got the name of his heroine) Leander seeks to persuade Hero that her chastity is, in effect, 'nothing':

> *This idol which you term Virginity,*
> *Is neither essence subject to the eye,*
> *No, nor to any one exterior sense,*
> *Nor hath it any place of residence,*
> *Nor is't of earth or mould celestial,*
> *Or capable of any form at all.*
> *Of that which hath no being do not boast,*
> *Things that are not at all are never lost.*
>
> (11.269–76)

The 'much ado' of Shakespeare's play is *about*, among other things, the question of Hero's chastity, and hence about the larger questions of marriage itself.

Themes

The themes of a Shakespeare play are the various connecting ideas which give unity and coherence to the dramatic action. *Much Ado About Nothing*, like nearly all of Shakespeare's comedies, is not explicitly concerned with issues like the tragic ironies attendant upon Man's realisation of his place in a universal scheme of things. Rather, its concerns are of a more domestic kind, dealing as it does with human relationships at a more down-to-earth social level, and particularly with the subject of marriage. Throughout the comedies, marriage is offered as the primary means whereby society renews itself, preserving continuity between one generation and the next, and affirming the very harmony upon which human society is founded. In *Much Ado About*

Nothing marriage is viewed from two perspectives, the one realistic, and the other romantic, and each is made, through the intricacies of the plot, to offer a comment on the other. The world of the play is not entirely free from 'evil', or indeed human contradiction, but the action moves steadily towards an exposure of the one, and an acceptance of the other, as major factors which comprise the life and vitality of society itself.

Throughout the play we are made aware of the discrepancy between what appears to be true and what is true, and we are in the privileged position so often typical of the audience of a comedy, of being able to watch the characters themselves as they act on the basis of information which they believe to be true but which we know is entirely false. This conflict between 'appearance' and 'reality', a pervasive theme to which Shakespeare returned in the major tragedies, is brought to bear on the actions of each of the major characters in the play, and is a constant source of comic irony; but unlike in, say, a tragedy like *Othello*, where its primary function is to reveal the wider moral perspective of the conflict between 'good' and 'evil', in *Much Ado About Nothing* it is enlisted in the service of *resolving* the difficulties which characters face, and of exposing and containing those forces harmful to the establishment and preservation of social harmony. Whereas in a tragedy like *Othello*, we are asked to sympathise fully with the plight of the hero as he submits himself finally to a judgement upon his actions, in *Much Ado About Nothing* characters such as Claudio are endowed neither with that sort of responsibility nor intensity.

John Russell Brown has observed that the structure of *Much Ado About Nothing*:

> depends almost entirely on one central theme, a theme which has already influenced parts of earlier comedies, that of appearance and reality, outward and inward beauty, words and thoughts—in short the theme of love's truth.*

Common to each of the play's major sources is a distinction between 'appearance' and 'reality', where the lover is tricked by some villainous form of deception. Love, the most fundamental of shared human emotions requires a degree of mutual trust, sincerity, commitment, and truth, but the theme which Professor Brown correctly identifies in this play extends far beyond the sphere of love-relationships as they appear in the comedies generally. Language, gesture, action, and appearance itself, are all means whereby characters come to 'know' each other, and, by implication, themselves, and this is a persistent concern in each of Shakespeare's plays. In *Much Ado About Nothing* the issue of deception—whether it be deception of others, as in the Claudio-Hero

*John Russell Brown, *Shakespeare's Comedies*, Methuen, London, 1957, p.121

plot, or self-deception, as is arguably the case in the Benedick-Beatrice plot—provides the foundation for an exploration of this more general theme.

From the outset, and particularly throughout the first scene of the play, we are made aware of the possible dangers inherent in relying entirely upon outward gestures and appearances, or indeed words themselves as the outward manifestation of thoughts. We learn, for example, that the valiant Claudio performed 'in the figure of a lamb, the feats of a lion' (I.1.13–14), to the point where language itself is not up to the task of describing his achievement: 'he hath indeed better bettered expectation than you must expect of me to tell you how' (I.1.14–15). Similarly, the Messenger's description of Claudio's uncle's response to his nephew's military achievements speaks of a joy 'that could not show itself modest enough without a badge of bitterness' (I.1.21–2); 'tears', the outward manifestation of grief, register in this context the feeling of 'joy', thus reinforcing the discrepancy between 'sign' and 'substance'. Leonato's reply ironically underscores this point:

a kind overflow of kindness; there are no faces truer than those that are so washed. How much better is it to weep at joy than joy at weeping. (I.1.24–6)

The irony of this remark is later deepened when in Act IV, Scene 1 Leonato refuses to apply this philosophy to Hero's gestures of innocence.

Beatrice's light-hearted but debilitating enquiries after Benedick lighten the tone of the dialogue, but even so, they pursue the same theme. Clearly, it would appear that in Messina, there is a degree of uncertainty about the relationship between 'seeming' and 'being', as Beatrice's audaciously witty remarks suggest; for example, in the field of military honour Benedick may be 'A lord to a lord, a man to a man, stuffed with all honourable virtues' (I.1.51–2) but Beatrice has her doubts about his inner qualities: 'he is no less than a stuffed man; but for the stuffing–well, we are all mortal' (I.1.53–4). For her Benedick's 'faith' is merely fashionable, and hence ephemeral: 'he wears his faith but as the fashion of his hat; it ever changes with the next block' (I.1.69–71), indicating that she believes that his inner convictions (faith) are really no more than an appearance (fashion). The more general point is made in a slightly different context later, when the villains Borachio and Conrade discuss 'fashion'; Borachio tells his accomplice: 'Thou knowest that the fashion of a doublet, or a hat, or a cloak, is nothing to a man' (III.3.114–16). The one serves to disguise rather than to reveal the other, hence 'fashion' is guilty of an act of deformity. The First Watchman's personification of the 'deformed thief' as 'Deformed' and Dogberry's more prolonged mangling of language itself reinforce, from a slightly different angle, the discrepancy between language and thought, where language itself possesses at least some of the attributes of 'fashion'.·

Public behaviour of all kinds in the play is open to more than one interpretation. For example, Beatrice claims that Benedick's presence is able to transform 'Courtesy itself' into 'disdain' (I.1.112–13) provoking from him the telling response that 'Then is courtesy a turncoat' (I.1.115), and thus consolidating the pervasive image of 'fashion' as an element in the wider dramatic conflict. The issue is raised in a slightly different guise when Don Pedro accepts Leonato's hospitality:

> I tell him we shall stay here at least a month, and he heartily prays some occasion may detain us longer. I dare swear he is no hypocrite, but prays from his heart. (I.1.140–3)

Here an implied distinction is being made between formal politeness on the one hand, and the sincere expression of genuine feeling on the other; Don Pedro trusts Leonato, but he expresses his view in such a way that our attention is drawn to the possibility of a disparity between language itself as a kind of outward appearance, and inner conviction, which in this case involves the reality of Leonato's own thoughts.

Usually it is Shakespeare's villains who forge a distinction between appearance and reality, characters such as Richard III, Claudius (*Hamlet*), or Iago (*Othello*), who habitually say one thing and think another. In *Much Ado About Nothing* the ethical implications of this ambiguity are not pursued (I.1.204), but his reply, 'By my troth, I speak my thought' (I.1.205) simply emphasises even more the difficulty raised by the notion of the uncertain relationship between appearances and reality itself. Moreover, the discrepancy between perspectives such as those of Benedick and Claudio is clearly a measure of the precariousness of judgements based upon appearances alone. What it does expose is that no matter how sincere particular characters are, that sincerity is always vulnerable to attack. These are, of course, the very grounds upon which Hero's sincerity will be attacked later in the play, and these small touches are a way of preparing us for it.

The parallel themes of human vulnerability on the one hand, and the discrepancy between appearance and reality on the other, remain central to the play. Attempting to judge by outward appearances can prove a hazardous affair, as Antonio's mistaken overhearing of the conversation between Claudio and Don Pedro proves to be. For him, the details he hears 'have a good cover, they show well outward' (I.2.6–7). Because we know that Antonio is mistaken, we appreciate the irony of his remark, but his mistake is an easy one to make, and is of the sort that will involve Claudio, Hero, Benedick, Beatrice, and Don Pedro in different ways later in the play. At this point, however, Leonato is cautious: 'We will hold it as a dream till it appear itself' (I.2.18–19), but this is caution *before* the event. Once the masque has taken place, the ineffectiveness of the men's disguises been easily penetrated, Don John has no difficulty in exploiting the limited awareness of others, and of persuading Claudio that Don Pedro has betrayed him. Remarkably, Claudio's response, once he hears the news, is to feel that in placing his trust in Don Pedro as his go-between, he is guilty of expecting constancy and loyalty in a matter which consistently furnishes proof to the contrary:

> *Friendship is constant in all other things*
> *Save in the office and affairs of love;*
> *Therefore all hearts in love use their own tongues.*
> *Let every eye negotiate for itself,*
> *And trust no agent; for beauty is a witch*
> *Against whose charms faith melteth into blood.*
> *This is an accident of hourly proof,*
> *Which I mistrusted not.*
>
> (II.1.160–7)

Don John's lie is all the more dangerous since it seems to have the support of 'experience', and even Benedick lends some credibility to it by suspecting Don Pedro (II.1.175–6). Similarly, the allegation against Hero, later, is based upon the notion that all women are unfaithful, a view to which Benedick himself subscribes for a large part of the play. Ironically both Claudio and Benedick are wrong in that they completely misjudge Don Pedro, and hence are open to the charge of being 'inexperienced'. In contrast with this superficial judgement of others, Friar Francis's observation of Hero after Claudio has openly rejected her is supported by a much more substantial kind of experience; while even Leonato misinterprets his daughter's reactions to her accusers as signs of her guilt, the Friar finds an alternative explanation, and one which we know to be true:

> *Trust not my reading nor my observations,*
> *Which with experimental seal doth warrant*
> *The tenor of my book; trust not my age,*
> *My reverence, calling, nor divinity,*
> *If this sweet lady lie not guiltless here*
> *Under some biting error.*
>
> (IV.1.163–8)

Friar Francis appeals to the 'trust' of those about him. And it is precisely this trust which Don John seeks to violate; indeed, in seeking to destroy trust between individuals he is attacking knowledge and with it the foundations of society itself. Benedick has to *trust* Beatrice's instincts about Hero's innocence, and Claudio has to place his trust completely in Leonato's ability to choose a wife for him.

This notion of mutual 'trust' is closely connected with another theme developed in the play, involving the extent to which 'time' and the experience which it brings both to Benedick and Claudio, changes their minds as they move from positions of ignorance, to ones of knowledge of themselves and of their respective partners. But it is Benedick rather than Claudio who provides the focus for this theme. Early in the play the more worldly Don Pedro ridicules Benedick's dogmatic stance against the institution of marriage, suggesting that in time he will change his mind. Beatrice has already had occasion to comment upon the ephemerality of Benedick's convictions (I.1.69–71), and in the conversation with Don Pedro, it is his 'faith' again which is at stake: 'Well, if ever thou dost fall from this faith, thou wilt prove a notable argument' (I.1.235–6). Moreover, with a philosophical ease, he dismisses Benedick's insistent arguments in favour of remaining a bachelor, with a crucial comment about the way in which 'time' and the experience which it brings, has the power to change people's minds: 'Well, as time shall try: 'In time the savage bull shall bear the yoke' (I.1.240–1). Don Pedro, Leonato, and the others actually arrange for Benedick to acquire the kind of experience which will make him change his mind, and much of the comedy in the play emanates from the exposure of the inconsistencies which result from their plot. Beatrice is subjected to a similar kind of experience, and she too changes.

The plot to bring them together, unlike the plot to separate Claudio and Hero from each other, is a constructive one, forcing them both into a position in which their inner feelings are required to harmonise with their outward behaviour. Ultimately, both acquire the courage of their convictions despite the fact that they know they will be ridiculed for being inconsistent. Right up until the end, the antagonism between feeling and outward behaviour is kept before us as Benedick's and Beatrice's writings are adduced as evidence against the public postures which they continue to maintain. It is Benedick himself who comments on the 'miracle' whereby these inconsistencies are exposed to view: 'Here's our own hands against our hearts' (V.4.91–2). But simply *saying* that time and experience have changed their minds is not enough since language itself has been consistently exposed in the play as a superficial counter capable of manipulation and distortion. Instead, Benedick seizes the initiative with a much more convincing gesture of affection which is, literally, beyond words: 'Peace! I will stop your mouth' (V.4.97). He then goes on to attack the predominantly intellectual positions which both he and Beatrice had occupied earlier, relinquishing his former dogmatic stance against women, for a more principled appreciation of them:

I'll tell thee what Prince; a college of wit-crackers cannot flout me out of my humour. Dost thou think that I care for a satire or an epigram? No; if a man will be beaten with brains, 'a shall wear nothing handsome about him. In brief, since I do purpose to marry, I will think nothing to any purpose that the world can say against it; therefore never flout at me for what I have said against it; for man is a giddy thing, and this is my conclusion.   (V.4.99–107)

Benedick's conclusion, his new-found appreciation of the contradictions inherent in human nature, is the result of an experience gained in 'time'. As with the Claudio–Hero plot, which functions on a much simpler level, it is 'time' and its theatrical adjunct 'timing' that ultimately reveal the truth of experience. In Benedick's view, criticism—which uses as its weapons in the play the 'satire' and the 'epigram'—must fulfil a positive function in that it should lead to a revaluation of Man's own many-sided nature. Significantly, Benedick does not relinquish 'fashion' as a potentially evil disguise (Borachio's position in Act III, Scene 3). Instead, he accepts the need to present a pleasing appearance, although this must not be allowed to displace the wider view that human beings are inconsistent by nature, and that, paradoxically, it is this inconsistency which is the source of their vitality.

The plots

Shakespearean comedy relies heavily on plot, and *Much Ado About Nothing* is no exception to this rule. Basically, the play consists of two parallel plots, each using similar ideas and situations, but moving in opposite directions. The Hero–Claudio plot is concerned with serious moral issues in that it is the force of 'evil', represented by the Bastard Don John, which seeks to destroy a love-relationship and with it the mutual trust upon which it should be based.

Alongside the Hero–Claudio plot, with its emphasis on romantic love, is the Beatrice–Benedick plot which begins realistically, and with mutual antagonism. Just as Claudio is the victim of a deception which causes him to change his mind, so both Beatrice and Benedick are deceived into changing their attitudes towards each other. Whereas in the one plot the movement involves one of attraction, separation, but final reunion, in the other, it begins with hostility and moves through a series of obstacles to a happy conclusion. Each plot can be broken down into a series of incidents all involving some form of disguise. For example, Don Pedro offers to woo Hero while disguised as Claudio, and Don John exploits Claudio's disguise to sow suspicion in his mind of Don Pedro's motives. Moreover, Antonio's imperfect overhearing allows Hero to prepare her disguise, but at the same time anticipates more wilful perversions of the truth later in the play. Similarly, the orchard scenes (II.3 and III.1) contain plays-within-plays in which groups of characters play particular roles for the benefit of their eavesdroppers.

Eavesdropping in the play is of two kinds. Firstly, there is the inaccurate overhearing of Antonio (I.2), and later on, the Watch (III.2), although both are unaware of the extent to which they mangle the truth, and in the latter case they are groping unsuspectingly towards it. Secondly, there are those scenes in which characters arrange for others to overhear them, and where the main motive is deception. In Act II, Scene 3, and Act III, Scene 1, the aim is to deceive Benedick and Beatrice into recognizing truths about themselves of which they seem to be unaware. But the plan arranged by Borachio and approved by Don John is designed to accomplish the opposite purpose with its combined use of disguise and eavesdropping. Thus, these plots, committed as they are to opposed sets of moral values, explore good and bad effects alternately.

With so much of the action depending upon disguise plots of one sort or another, it is hardly necessary to act out on stage the deceiving of Claudio, the central action towards which all the other plot strands converge. From the consequences of Claudio's public rejection of Hero emerge the seeds of the final resolution. Nonetheless, one or two difficulties are raised by the plot to make public Hero's death, and some critics have seen in Act V, Scene 1 some ambiguity in the seemingly indulgent behaviour of both Leonato and Antonio. Both know that Hero is alive, and yet their headstrong expressions of grief and anger at Claudio's action seem to go some way beyond that demanded by the parts that they are called upon to act. In one sense, their seriousness, along with the parallel case of Benedick who, like Antonio, also issues a challenge to Claudio, is offset by what we already know of the imminent discovery of the facts surrounding Claudio's rejection of Hero. Also, if Leonato and Antonio *are* acting a part, convincing though it is, it contrasts with Benedick's seriousness which is based upon his own trust of Beatrice's instincts about Hero's innocence. Unlike the other two, Benedick, as we know, has something very specific to prove by making this challenge. Benedick's challenge bridges the gap between the two plots, and in doing so helps to further one of the play's major thematic concerns, that of the relationship between 'sign' and 'substance'.

It is not until Act V that these various plot strands begin to knit together. Up until this point each movement in the serious plot to undermine Claudio's faith in Hero is undercut by the comic scenes involving Dogberry and Verges. These comic episodes extend the treatment of some of the play's main themes, and they also contain the solution to the problem posed by Don John and his accomplices. The fact that the information they possess is held back enables Shakespeare to introduce a measure of dramatic tension into the action, while at the same time reassuring us that a happy resolution will, in the fullness of time, be achieved. The manipulation of particular characters continues right up until Act V, Scene 3 where Claudio and Don John play a part without realizing that they are doing so, but the 'resurrection' of Hero can only take place once all the details in both plots have been fully synchronised, and each of the characters involved is in the correct frame of mind. The final stage grouping and the dance which follows, reinforce the idea of harmony towards which the action has been steadily moving.

Setting

Although Shakespeare could and did present pictures of low urban life in his plays (*Measure For Measure* (1604) is perhaps a good example), he seems to have been more generally concerned with love-relationships and with 'romantic' sentiment. Invariably, comic plots in Shakespeare have a 'domestic' setting, and hinge upon violations of friendship, and hence loyalty, parental opposition to the marriages of their children, and the extent to which inconsistencies in behaviour arise in human affairs generally. These obstacles are required to be overcome before a happy conclusion can be reached, and in almost every case (*Love's Labours Lost* (1595) is perhaps, an exception) the final scene brings with it a new-found harmony which provides the basis for society's renewal of itself. In *Much Ado About Nothing*, the status of individual characters ranges from the princely Don Pedro to the most menial member of the Watch, but although human folly is the mainspring of the action, the play does not dwell exclusively upon it for purposes of satire only. This variety is reflected in the play's 'language' which ranges from the stylised utterances of characters like Claudio to the confused colloquialism of Dogberry or Verges, each having a part to play in the overall design.

Here the attention is focused upon one particular household, that of Leonato, Governor of Messina, and more specifically upon the relationships between his daughter and his niece, on the one hand, and Claudio and Benedick on the other. But Messina is a topsy-turvy world where justice itself seems somehow deficient. At least, with the possible exception of Benedick, who guesses at the source of malice in the play:

> *Two of them have the very bent of honour;*
> *And if their wisdoms be misled in this,*
> *The practice of it lives in John the Bastard,*
> *Whose spirits toil in frame of villainies.*
> (IV.1.184–7)

Few of the characters seem able to cope with the difficulties which arise. In what seems a fair criticism of at least some of the aristocratic characters in the play, Borachio, one of Don John's accomplices, says: 'What your wisdoms could not discover, these shallow fools have brought to light' (V.1.221–2). Clearly 'wisdom' in the play is vulnerable; in the cases of Claudio and Don Pedro, and to some extent Leonato himself, it can be misled, while in the cases of Benedick and Beatrice it is misleading, in the sense that their superficial grasp of the realities of human relationships actually blinds them to their own deficiencies. Each claims to possess wisdom culled from experience, but each has overlooked their own inconsistencies; Claudio is not 'wise' enough to distinguish Hero from popular notions of female inconstancy, nor are Leonato and Antonio wise enough to be able to deal rationally with the situation which Don John's mischief has created. In this comedy 'evil', in the form of the 'illegitimate' Don John, is kept at bay; it is a force in human affairs which has to be *discovered*, and although we are given a brief glimpse of it in action, its power is already undermined by the revelations in Act III, Scene 3, which the Watch—the most menial group in the play—are privileged to overhear. Indeed, whatever we may say about Dogberry and the Watch, their notion of 'justice' seems far more effective in its own way than that of their superiors, in that it actually brings the correct results.

With the aid of Friar Francis, whose standards of judgement are correct, the final movement is initiated whereby Hero is brought back to life (something which in the later play, *Othello,* can never happen to Desdemona), and the evil which caused her 'death' is exposed before any lasting harm can be done. The celebratory dance at the end of the play proclaims that a new kind of social harmony has been discovered, one which takes into full account the contradictions in human nature, and in this climate, the evil which Don John represents is reduced to a matter not worth thinking about:

> *Think not on him till tomorrow; I'll devise*
> *thee brave punishments for him. Strike up, pipers.*
> (V.4.125–6)

As a physical setting for the play, Messina has no particular significance, except that Shakespeare is following closely his source in Bandello's novella. But as a reflection of the pyschological landscape of its characters, it offers us an image of an entire society, and of its progress towards a new, more harmonious vision of itself.

Character and characterisation

Let us now turn to the question of character. It is not surprising, given Shakespeare's impressive grasp of the complexities of human affairs, that the characters he draws should engage our attention as full individuals, of the kind that we sometimes find in novels. On the other hand, to react too strongly against this, as some critics have done, and to view all characters as 'types', is to fail to give full credit to Shakespeare's considerable powers of characterisation. The difficulty is increased in *Much Ado About Nothing*, and in the Comedies generally, where we are made constantly aware of the mechanics of plotting, and the extent to which the characters are being manipulated for primarily dramatic purposes; but even here some attempt is made to relate their individuality to their function as contributors to the action which the playwright seeks to present. For example, Don John is clearly a one-dimensional character, driven by a particular 'humour' or bent of mind, and committed only to the pursuit of mischief. To this extent he is a 'plot device', although it must be admitted that he is Don Pedro's brother, and he is motivated by a complex of recognisable, though not easily explicable, human impulses. To take two more complex examples, Hero and Beatrice have 'literary' pedigrees in addition to what they possess as individualised characters. Hero is the literary 'type' of contancy in love, drawing at least some of her vitality from her original in Marlowe's poem *Hero and Leander*, while Beatrice may have her 'literary' origins in the Italian medieval poet Dante's Beatrice in *The Divine Comedy* who is the 'blessedness' to which the poet aspires. But Shakespeare is not satisfied with creating them merely as 'types', literary or otherwise. Hero's emotions are vivid and convincing, growing out of the situations in which she is placed, while Beatrice's realistic and earthy appraisal of human relationships makes any possible connection with Dante's 'heavenly' Beatrice ironical to say the least. Similarly, Benedick, whose name also means 'blessed', is an amalgam of recognisable human contradictions, which reach out beyond the requirements of plot, although it is true to say that at the end of the play both he and Beatrice attain an objective which would be described as 'blessed' in that they finally submit themselves to love, and to marriage.

Claudio

At first sight Claudio seems a conventionally 'romantic' character, and in some respects this is a role he fulfils within the larger design of the play. Even before he appears on stage, he is praised by the Messenger who reports that his achievements in the recent battle were extraordinary for one of his age:

He hath borne himself beyond the promise of his age, doing, in the figure of a lamb, the feats of a lion; he hath indeed better bettered expectation than you must expect of me to tell you how.

(I.1.12–15)

and later, as 'the right noble Claudio' he refers to him (I.1.78).

When Claudio enters, with Don Pedro, Benedick and Don John, he says nothing, but evidently the mere sight of Hero turns his thoughts to romance. His first words to Benedick, after everyone else has left the stage, establish a contrast between the points of view of the two characters, and forms the basis of an important dramatic tension sustained throughout the play: 'Benedick, didst thou note the daughter of Signior Leonato?' (I.1.152). Claudio's affection for Hero is serious enough to prompt him to consider breaking all former promises: 'I would scarce trust myself, though I had sworn the contrary, if Hero would be my wife' (I.1.182–3), although in the light of Benedick's cynical dismissal of the institution of marriage generally, his position is made to seem an extreme one. But when we consider the change of heart that Benedick will himself be forced to undergo later, our attitude to Claudio's romantic infatuation is softened considerably. Serious though his attraction to Hero is, we cannot help noticing the irony of the remark he makes about his changing passions: 'If my passion change not shortly, God forbid it should be otherwise!' (I.1.202). The dialogue with Don Pedro in Act I, Scene 1 raises further doubts in our minds. Indeed, some critics have interpreted Claudio's question: 'Hath Leonato any son, my lord?' (I.1.273) as evidence of a mercenary interest in inheritance, but when we remember that in Elizabethan times marriage (usually arranged by parents) was as much a financial transaction as an affair of the heart, then Claudio's question seems perfectly in order. In any event, he goes on to tell Don Pedro of his own feelings for Hero, although we may register in passing the impression that love itself is a precarious business, and lovers changeable and irrational in their attitudes:

> O, my lord,
> When you went onward on this ended action,
> I looked upon her with a soldier's eye,
> That liked, but had a rougher task in hand
> Than to drive liking to the name of love;
> But now I am returned and that war-thoughts
> Have left their places vacant, in their rooms
> Come thronging soft and delicate desires,
> All prompting me how fair young Hero is,
> Saying I liked her ere I went to wars.

(I.1.275–84)

The romantic tone of Claudio's speech is unmistakable, and Don Pedro immediately recognises his friend's conventional posture: 'Thou wilt be like a lover presently/And tire the hearer with a book of words' (I.1.285–6). While we do not doubt the genuineness of Claudio's expression of love for Hero, the fact that, by his own admission, he has already changed his mind once, leads us to ask whether he fully knows himself.

Claudio may have doubts about trusting himself in certain situations, but he trusts Don Pedro to act as a go-between in securing Hero, and it is this faith in others which the villainous Don John manages to undermine. To some extent Claudio lacks the depth of experience to determine accurately the motives of others, although he has no reason to believe in Don Pedro's alleged treachery; indeed, his rationalisations are no more than commonplace attitudes which in no way reflect his personal experience of Don Pedro's friendship. His application of commonplace observations to the behaviour of particular individuals whom he knows, has the effect of temporarily distorting his knowledge of them, but we must bear in mind that Claudio is not the only one who is misled in this way in the play. The new 'knowledge' which Don John cunningly reveals to him stifles his loquacity, as the comparative sullenness of his attitude in the dialogue which follows, indicates. Thus Claudio relinquishes the 'wordy' role of conventional romantic lover, for that of the silent and melancholy jealous man, and it is the shrewd Beatrice who observes this change:

> The Count is neither sad, nor sick, nor merry, nor well; but civil count, civil as an orange, and something of that jealous complexion.
> (II.1.269–71)

This mood is, however, short-lived since the suspicion engendered by Don John, and inadvertently supported by Benedick, concerning Don Pedro's loyalty is publicly disproved. Claudio now registers the new firmness of his relationship with Hero with a different kind of silence, for despite Beatrice's urging him to speak: 'Speak, Count, 'tis your cue' (II.1.281), he chooses a more effective kind of communication than words, one which foreshadows Benedick's own behaviour in Act V, Scene 4: 'Silence is the perfectest herald of joy; I were but little happy if I could say how much.' (II.1.282–3). Having now disproved commonplace notions concerning trust and fidelity in courtship, Claudio now seems in a unassailable position, and it is with this confidence that he participates in the plot to bring Benedick and Beatrice together. But his situation remains an ironical one. Now the very strength of his commitment to Hero, combined with the more general uncertainty that pervades the atmosphere of Messina, will be used by Don John and Borachio against him. The irony of his position deepens when he begins to adopt the witty posture vacated by Benedick as he is persuaded to change his mind about Beatrice.

Although it is fairly clear that the character of Claudio is being influenced for dramatic purposes, his public rejection of Hero in Act IV, Scene 1 seems harsh. It raises questions about the extent to which he actually did 'trust' Hero in the first place, although again the play does not dwell for any length of time upon the psychological effects of this rejection upon Claudio. His rejection of Hero reminds us of his behaviour in Act II, Scene 1, where subsequent experience of Don Pedro's loyalty disproved the commonplace truths which Claudio had mistakenly adduced in support of his suspicions. Perhaps we can accuse Claudio of single-minded impetuosity, although both he and Don Pedro have actually seen proof (so they think) of Hero's infidelity. But again, Claudio is not alone in his response. In addition to Don Pedro, Leonato quickly believes that Hero is guilty, suggesting that the naivety embodied in Claudio is shared by others in the play.

Claudio's responses to each situation are shown to be instinctive; he reacts first, and rationalises after, hence the impression he creates throughout of lacking real experience. What we can be certain of, however, is the sheer intensity of his emotional responses. He does not disgrace Hero out of pique; he is genuinely upset, and it is the outward manifestation of his grief to which Leonato refers in an attempt to determine the sincerity of his action:

> Would the two princes lie, and Claudio lie,
> Who loved her so, that, speaking of her foulness,
> Washed it with tears?

(IV.1.150–2)

When Claudio next appears in Act V, Scene 1, it is to defend his honour against Leonato (who still does not know the full story behind Claudio's rejection of her), and Benedick, whose challenge will provide proof of his commitment to Beatrice. Again with Don Pedro's support, Claudio's encounter with Leonato and Antonio is short and to the point, revealing more about the characters of his adversaries than about his own, but when faced with Benedick he resumes the role of witty rationalist that the latter has relinquished.

With the entry of Dogberry and Borachio, Claudio undergoes yet another change as he is made to realise the full enormity of his action in rejecting Hero. There is a sense in which Claudio's responses are being manipulated in accordance with the general plan formulated by Friar Francis in Act IV, Scene 1. Also, we know that Hero is not dead, and this too prevents Claudio from fully engaging our sympathies at this point. Nonetheless. his reaction to Borachio's news is intense: 'I have drunk poison whiles he uttered it' (V.1.232), and, grief-stricken, he now places his fate in the hands of Leonato:

> *O noble sir!*
> *Your over-kindness doth wring tears from me.*
> *I do embrace your offer, and dispose*
> *For henceforth of poor Claudio.*
>
> (V.1.279–82)

We also know, of course, that this final expression of trust will culminate in a happy reunion with Hero. Claudio's enactment of the mourning ritual in Act V, Scene 3, and his blind acceptance of the wife Leonato has chosen for him, reinforces the extent to which he can now, with confidence, be a man of his word. Claudio's 'sin' has been one of 'mistaking' (V.1.262), but, however, his attitude has in no way been wilful, and there is a clear sense in which the burden of his 'sin' is shared by all the other characters in the play who are themselves victims of deceit.

Hero

Hero's character presents us with fewer difficulties of interpretation, and, in addition, her name suggests an explicit 'literary' comparison with the heroine of Marlowe's poem, providing an ironic gloss on the role she plays. Hero is a faithful mistress accused wrongly of infidelity, yet she is not above engaging in certain forms of deception. In other respects, she is a conventional daughter, obedient to her father's wishes, and lacking in independence. Hero is not allowed, in the early stages of the play, to reveal herself, hence the impression she creates upon others varies from individual to individual, as the opposed responses of Benedick and Claudio indicate (see I.1.152–3).

Hero does not actually speak until Act II, Scene 1, but already our impression of her is that of a dutiful daughter. As a preface to her brief encounter with the disguised Don Pedro, her cousin Beatrice observes the extent of her submission to parental authority:

> Yes, faith; it is my cousin's duty to make curtsy and say, 'Father as it please you'. But yet for all that, cousin, let him be a handsome fellow, or else make another curtsy and say, 'Father, as it please me.'
>
> (II.1.46–9)

She emerges from the encounter with Don Pedro with credit, having controlled the dialogue with heavily ironic comments on the nature of his disguise. In each of the brief dialogues which follow, the women get the better of their partners, although in Hero's case, the situation has been prepared for her beforehand by her father.

Claudio's crisis of faith in Don Pedro, and its resolution, provokes no comment whatsoever from Hero, although it is perhaps reasonable to assume that once his faith in others is restored, she proffers a gesture of affection towards him, although it is on Beatrice's instruction:

Speak, cousin; or, if you cannot, stop his mouth with a kiss, and let him not speak neither. (II.1.286–7)

By contrast, in Act V, Scene 4, Benedick needs no prompting for such a gesture. At the end of Act II, Scene 1 Hero seems prepared to participate in a plan, devised by someone else (Don Pedro), although at the same time it is her 'modesty' and dutifulness which are emphasised: 'I will do any modest office, my lord, to help my cousin to a good husband' (II.1.347–8). Thus Hero is established early on as a character who is conventional in her behaviour, somewhat reticent, and yet eager to help others provided that her 'modesty' and 'duty' are in no way compromised.

From Act III, Scene 1 onwards, Hero's character is sketched in a little more fully, with emphasis being placed upon the irony of her situation. The formal poetic language and verse dialogue of the scene contrast with the prose of the preceding scene, and help to create a 'romantic' context for the deception of Beatrice. Her ornate poetic description of the orchard and its 'pleached bower' (III.1.7ff.) set the scene and reinforce what we already know of the conventional nature of Hero's role. But the irony emerges when in sketching out the plan with Ursula, she seems much more aware than either Benedick or Beatrice of the extent to which language itself can prove deceptive:

> Of this matter
> Is little Cupid's crafty arrow made,
> That only wounds by hearsay.

(III.1.21–3)

She is aware of the 'false sweet bait' (III.1.33) with which Beatrice is to be trapped, and she knows also how proud and self-centred her cousin is. Though ultimately Hero is committed to truth and simplicity, her knowledge of Beatrice's character indicates that she is not naive, although she seems naturally to be compassionate. She objects to Beatrice's distortions of the qualities of others, and she argues for a more straightforward appreciation of human merit:

> So turns she every man the wrong side out,
> And never gives to truth and virtue that
> Which simpleness and merit purchaseth.

(III.1.68–70)

Up until Act III, Scene 4, Hero engages little of our sympathy. She is weak enough to be influenced by her father, and Don John succeeds in persuading Claudio, albeit temporarily, that she will succumb to Don Pedro's allegedly selfish advances. But as we learn more about Borachio's plot, so we become more sympathetic to Hero's plight. She comes nearest to arousing our sympathies in Act III, Scene 4 where she innocently prepares for her wedding. And yet, despite her earlier commitment to 'truth' and 'simplicity' she rejects Margaret's bluntness in pointing out some of the sexual facts of her forthcoming marriage. Hero's 'modesty' acts as a barrier between her and the truth, and her propriety is thus made to seem like an empty posture alongside Margaret's frankness:

> Is not marriage honourable in a beggar? Is not your lord honourable without marriage? I think you would have me say 'saving your reverence, a husband': an bad thinking do not wrest true speaking, I'll offend nobody. Is there any harm in 'the heavier for a husband'? None, I think, an it be the right husband and the right wife; otherwise 'tis light, and not heavy: (III.4.26–33)

Unlike Beatrice, Hero does not change in the play. Natural though her conventional attitude is, her deficiencies are highlighted by juxtaposing her rigidity of mind with Beatrice's capacity for change, as the dialogues between her and Margaret, and Margaret and Beatrice indicate. In Act IV, Scene 1 in which she is publicly rejected, Hero still holds on to the attitude which was exposed in the preceding scene. Confronted with Claudio's relentless attack, she responds with a comment about the impropriety of his language: 'Is my lord well, that he doth speak so wide?' (IV.1.60). In this instance Hero is right and Claudio is wrong, and consequently her vulnerability attracts our sympathy. But her swooning (apart from being an imitation of the act of death) underlines the extent to which she can only respond to situations created by others, and this is the role that she occupies for the remainder of the play.

Benedick

Benedick's role counterbalances that of Claudio, and as with the other major figures in the play, we are interested in what others say about him as much as in what he reveals of his own character. Beatrice is scathing about him, although her point of view is considered to be a distorted one, but even so, her allegation that he is 'changeable' receives some corroboration from his behaviour later. When Beatrice claims that 'he wears his faith but as the fashion of his hat; it ever changes with the next block' (I.1.69–71), she intends to convey the impression that Benedick is wholly without substance, although the events of Act

II, Scene 3 show that he is capable of changing for the better:

I did never think to marry. I must not seem proud; happy are they
that hear their detractions and can put them to mending. They say
the lady is fair; 'tis a truth, I can bear them witness; and virtuous;
so, I cannot reprove it; and wise, but for loving me. By my troth, it
is no addition to her wit, nor no great argument of her folly, for I will
be horribly in love with her. I may chance have some odd quirks and
remnants of wit broken on me, because I have railed so long against
marriage; but doth not the appetite alter? A man loves the meat in
his youth that he cannot endure in his age.   (II.3.223–32)

From this point onwards, Benedick shows some private awareness of
the contradictions in his own character, and he endears himself to us
by devaluing, slightly, his own qualities. But much of the plot is
concerned with the public exposure of these contradictions. Moreover,
his change of heart is prompted by a deception of which he is unaware,
and his rationalisation of his position is too glib to be wholly convincing,
although we are far more sympathetic to him than we are to, say,
Claudio.

Benedick's character consists of two basic strands; firstly he is noted
for his public attitude towards women, as indicated by his general
pronouncements, by his attitude towards Beatrice and by the 'skirmishes
of wit' in which they are both involved. These 'skirmishes' are essentially
destructive in that each character is concerned to gain a victory over
the other. In these scenes (I.1, and II.1) Benedick acts after his 'custom,
as being a professed tyrant' (I.1.159) to women generally, although he
admits that he is also 'an honest man' who possesses a 'simple true
judgement' (I.1.157–8). His hostility to women stems from a deep
distrust of their loyalty and fidelity, and he maintains during the early
part of the play, that marriage inevitably brings discredit upon the man:

That a woman conceived me, I thank her; that she brought me up,
I likewise give her most humble thanks; but that I will have a recheat
winded in my forehead, or hang my bugle in an invisible baldrick, all
women shall pardon me. Because I will not do them the wrong to
mistrust any, I will not do myself the right to trust none.
(I.1.220–6)

Benedick's fear is born out of a selfish mistrust, and in the first two acts
of the play, his self-interest and the defensiveness it engenders, indicates
that he would be unsuitable for the sorts of demands which marriage
would place upon him. His persistent adherence to commonplace truths
shows that he lacks personal experience, so that his wit, attractive
though it may seem on the surface, is both shallow and destructive. The
wiser Don Pedro is less sanguine about Benedick's ability to hang on

to his professed viewpoint: 'Well, if ever thou dost fall from this faith, thou wilt prove a notable argument' (I.1.234–5), hinting that his 'faith' has more in common with Beatrice's view of it than his own.There is a sense in these early scenes that Benedick is deluded into believing that he knows his own mind, although others, notably Don Pedro, have a much shrewder appreciation of it.

In certain respects Benedick resembles Hero in that the situation in which his grasp of the truth places him is both ironical, reflecting upon his character, and advances the plot of the play. His prose soliloquy at the beginning of Act II, Scene 3, comparing his attitude to Claudio's, seeks to establish his own cynical and misogynistic rejection of romance in favour of an honest plainness:

> He was wont to speak plain and to the purpose, like an honest man and a soldier, and now is he turned orthography; his words are a very fantastical banquet, just so many strange dishes. May I be so converted and see with these eyes? I cannot tell; I think not.
> (II.3.18–22)

His analysis of the extreme which Claudio represents is accurate, and yet, by the end of the scene he changes his mind and observes 'some marks of love' in Beatrice (II.3.238) where, clearly, on the basis of what she actually says, none exists. The joke lies in the fact that Benedick has been caught in his own plot, but the matter does not end with his private reversal of attitude. Marriage involves certain public, as well as private, obligations, and when the plot to bring Beatrice and Benedick together is taken up again in Act IV, it is with a renewed sense of what those obligations involve. It is not sufficient for Benedick to adopt the tone of the romantic lover that he does upon hearing of Beatrice's affections for him: 'Fair Beatrice I thank you for your pains' (II.3.241). A change of utterance from prose to blank verse is meaningless without a change of attitude generally, and Beatrice's 'Kill Claudio' (IV.1.285), extravagant though it is, is designed to accomplish just that.

The context in which Benedick is asked to 'Kill Claudio' helps to reduce the potential seriousness of the request. Beatrice rants nervously, and Benedick is denied the opportunity of speaking at all, but the subject of her withering contempt is the man of 'appearances', the formal man who is wholly without substance:

> But manhood is melted into curtsies, valour into compliment, and men are only turned into tongue, and trim ones too. He is now as valiant as Hercules that only tells a lie and swears it. I cannot be a man with wishing, therefore I will die a woman with grieving.
> (IV.1.313–18)

Benedick's romantically exaggerated gesture of commitment—'Come, bid me do anything for thee' (IV.1.284)—is now fully exposed for what it is, and he is forced to think seriously about his attitude to Beatrice. The turning-point comes with his decision to 'trust' her instincts in a way that he has never trusted any woman before: 'Think you in your soul the Count Claudio hath wronged Hero?' (IV.1.323). Moreover, the seriousness of the challenge he subsequently issues is made to contrast with the witty cynicism of Claudio, (who has, as Beatrice had predicted earlier, 'caught the Benedick' (I.1.82)) and the outrageously irrational attitudes of Leonato and Antonio.

In Act V, Scene 2 Benedick tries and fails to eulogise his mistress in poetry. Although, as we have seen, his language changes as his attitude changes, the status occupied by language in the play as a form of 'appearance' prevents him from automatically adopting the formal 'romantic' utterance of Claudio. Indeed, no amount of 'literary' analogy will adequately express his inner feelings for Beatrice:

> but in loving, Leander the good swimmer, Troilus the first employer of panders, and a whole bookful of these quondam carpet-mongers, whose names yet run smoothly in the even road of a blank verse, why, they were never so truly turned over and over as my poor self in love. Marry, I cannot show it in rhyme, I have tried; (V.2.30–6)

and he concludes: 'No, I was not born under a rhyming planet, nor I cannot woo in festival terms' (V.2.39–40). And yet, in the final scene of the play it is his 'halting sonnet of his own pure brain' (V.4.87) which publicly exposes the genuineness of his affection for Beatrice. His rejection of 'wit' and cynicism and his conclusion that 'man is a giddy thing' (V.4.106) constitutes, in effect, a commitment to live in the fullness of knowledge, and at the same time to resolve to distinguish between positive and negative attitudes.

Beatrice

Beatrice's role in the play is similar to that of Benedick, except that certain issues that affect them both are placed in a clearer focus in her character. Unlike Hero, who is dominated from the outset by her father Leonato's wishes, Beatrice has an independence of mind accorded to no other female character in the play. She intends, as she tells her less forceful cousin, to please herself in marriage (II.1.46–9), and to this extent she is less of a victim of circumstance in the play than Hero. Unlike Dante's Beatrice, who exemplifies a 'blessed' state towards which the poet aspires, Shakespeare's Beatrice has her feet very firmly on the ground. However, she and Benedick—both of whom exemplify at the end of the play the 'blessed' state of matrimony—work towards a relationship which has all the signs of proving successful, and in which each partner has an equal status with the other.

Beatrice's realistic attitude, however, requires closer examination, particularly in the light of the criticisms that are levelled against her by others in the play. Shakespeare leaves us to wonder whether she is in love with Benedick from the outset; it is true that she questions the Messenger about his exploits: 'I pray you, sir, is Signior Mountanto returned from the wars, or no?' (I.1.28–9), although it is clear from the tone of her request that the prevailing attitude she adopts is one of contempt. In the early stages of the play Beatrice casts Benedick in the role of fashionable braggart occupied with appearances only, but he responds with the allegation—also containing more than a grain of truth—that she is a chatterer: 'I would my horse had the speed of your tongue, and so a good continuer' (I.1.132–3); later he leaves as she enters with the comment: 'O God, sir, here's a dish I love not; I cannot endure my Lady Tongue' (II.1.251–2). Beatrice, like Benedick, initially displays an indiscriminate use of words, and as such they both unwittingly distort the objects they describe. Beatrice may 'apprehend passing shrewdly', and we may believe that she has a 'good eye, uncle; I can see a church by daylight' (II.1.71–2), but what begins as realism on her part frequently borders on cynical disdain.

Beatrice's insistence that she will remain unmarried is a mark of arrogant superiority, in addition to providing a timely challenge to Don Pedro and the others, and she is made to pass through the same changes of outlook as her future partner. In the Masque Beatrice reports what she knows to be Benedick's criticisms of her: 'That I was disdainful, and that I had my wit out of the "Hundred Merry Tales"—well, this was Signior Benedick that said so' (II.1.115–17), yet she refuses to heed this analysis, rejecting it out of hand as one of those 'impossible slanders' that she believes he delights in formulating (II.1.124). In one sense, just as Benedick has 'seen' but not *noticed* Hero, so Beatrice is being invited to look at her faults, but fails to take any notice of them. Rather, she chooses to attack Benedick's point of view, having, it would seem, already penetrated his disguise. But her knowledge is no less adequate than that of her adversary, and perceptive though she can be in certain situations (note her recognition of the signs of jealousy in Claudio: II.1.269–71), she seems unable to discriminate clearly between a realistic outlook and a distortion of the facts.

The more dogmatic Beatrice's stance in the early stages of the play, the greater will be the comic impact of her change of heart when it comes. Interestingly, Hero's fabricated criticisms of her character are much harsher than Don Pedro's of Benedick's, testifying perhaps to the relatively superior position that she occupies in the play. Her distortion of human qualities and her refusal to give 'to truth and virtue that/Which simpleness and merit purchaseth' (III.1.70–1), along with her total unwillingness to share love, are serious deficiencies, which receive an added emphasis from her demonstration of hostility to an already weakened Benedick in the preceding scene (II.3.239ff.). Hero and her ladies-in-waiting use Beatrice's pride against her, and the ploy proves successful in persuading her to change. Under the guise of an artificially contrived situation (through which Benedick and Beatrice fail to see), certain truths emerge which will require a change of outlook.

From Act III, Scene 1 onwards, Beatrice relinquishes her 'wit' to the point where in Act III, Scene 4 she can rebuke Margaret for having acquired it, just as she objects to her chattering: 'What a pace is this that thy tongue keeps?' (III.4.84). Only when she sees her faults in others can she recognise them, but even this raises problems. Beatrice's change from one attitude to another is extreme, and Margaret's reply: 'Not a false gallop' (III.4.85) draws our attention to the accuracy of her criticism. As with Benedick, Beatrice is not required to replace pessimistic disdain with romantic optimism; indeed, the play suggests that neither seems a good basis upon which to build a marriage. Rather, she has to experience vicariously the effects of mistrust which others reveal before she can finally commit herself.

The public disgracing of Hero provides the opportunity to consolidate this change of attitude. Beatrice may not trust men, and the harshness of Claudio's exposure of his bride weakens any incentive to do so, but she is prepared to trust Hero's integrity. Indeed, this incident serves to reveal a depth of emotion in Beatrice which has hitherto remained hidden. Benedick's question: 'Lady Beatrice, have you wept all this while?' (IV.1.253) draws our attention to a gesture easily observable in performance, which speaks more eloquently than language itself. When she does begin to express her feelings she extravagantly attacks the male propensity to divorce language from action; the dual effect of this is to reveal her own distress, surprising for someone who has hitherto always had total control of her feelings, but it also effectively traps Benedick into proving the substantiality of his love for her. Nor, as the dialogue in Act V, Scene 2 shows, will she be satisfied with anything that falls short of complete commitment from him.

Beatrice's demand that Benedick 'Kill Claudio', is, of course, an unreasonable one, but it marks a change from her earlier prodigal use of language, to an absurdly literal respect for it. When she asks Benedick to account for himself in Act V, Scene 2, she demonstrates exactly how extreme the change has been, as she resumes for a moment the 'witty' posture which she had earlier relinquished. When Benedick reports that 'Only foul words' passed between him and Claudio (V.2.47)—an understatement of the facts—she refuses to allow him to kiss her, a rebuff which draws from him a telling response: 'Thou has frighted the word out of his right sense, so forcible is thy wit' (V.2.51–2). It would seem that Beatrice's commitment to literal meaning (she has, we should remember, always held a healthy regard for consistency in others) is almost as devastating in its distortion of the facts as her witty disdain had been. But they both appear to have disproved the validity of 'wit' itself; though they resort briefly to witty postures, they are finally forced to admit to each other that they are both 'ill' (V.2.81–3), a blunt acknowledgement which proves more convincing than all the verbal evasions and romantic formulations which precede it. It is in the final scene of the play that Beatrice and Benedick are forced to admit publicly to the feelings that they express privately to each other in Act V, Scene 2. As a residually defensive measure they try to resort to familiar public postures, but Beatrice's confidence is quickly undermined by Hero's producing the 'evidence' of her affection for Benedick. She too, it seems, writes 'A halting sonnet,' indicating that she is not entirely comfortable adopting a romantic posture either. But just as she begins to justify her behaviour, with what looks like a reversion to the disdain that she had abandoned, Benedick seizes the initiative and kisses her, thus making an explanation superfluous. His 'Peace. I will stop your mouth' (V.4.97) literally returns to its source Beatrice's earlier advice to Hero (II.1.286–7), and she is finally silenced in a gesture of mutual affection which happily exposes the inadequacy of words. In the character of Beatrice (as in that of Benedick) Shakespeare has succeeded in combining psychological fullness with the demands of plot.

Don Pedro

Don Pedro is responsible for carrying a large part of each of the two plots. He returns victorious from a war in which Claudio has distinguished himself, and he offers to act as a go-between in the younger man's first approach to Hero. When he first appears he comments upon the lavish preparations which Leonato has made to entertain him, conveying the impression that he is considerate of the endeavours of others: 'Good Signior Leonato, are you come to meet your trouble? The fashion of the world is to avoid cost and you encounter it' (I.1.89–91). Moreover, he is also sufficiently aware of the ways of the world to be able to distinguish between its qualities and its deficiencies; for example, his confidence in Leonato's sincerity is expressed in terms of trust, while revealing that not everyone can be trusted: 'I dare swear he is no hypocrite, but prays from his heart' (I.1.142–3).

In a conversation with Benedick, later in Act I, Scene 1, he demonstrates the extent of his own experience in worldly matters. Benedick swears that he will never marry, but Don Pedro knows that in time he will change his mind (I.1.235–6). Similarly, in his conversation with

Claudio he shows that he knows how to 'read' others, usually in a sympathetic manner:

> *What need the bridge much broader than the flood?*
> *The fairest grant is the necessity.*
> *Look what will serve is fit. 'Tis once, thou lovest,*
> *And I will fit thee with the remedy.*
>
> (I.1.295–8)

It is out of Don Pedro's natural desire to help Claudio that the first stage of the plot to deceive him is formulated.

In the scene in which he and the others dupe Benedick, his analysis of the victim's psychology is accurate but not harsh. Benedick's extravert wit is, he suggests, the product of an attempt to cover up his real feelings: 'for the man doth fear God, howsoever it seems not in him by some large jests he will make' (II.3.94–6). This plot begins as a game designed to occupy the time between Claudio's engagement and the actual marriage, but it turns out to contain more 'matter' than even Don Pedro had hoped for, since not only do Benedick's and Beatrice's 'opinions' of each other produce 'merely a dumb-show' (II.3.213–14), but the two finally come together in a union which has all the signs of proving strong.

Having set this plot in motion, Don Pedro, with the help of others, extracts the full comic irony from Benedick's predicament as the dialogue in Act III, Scene 2 indicates (3.2.1–67). But this legitimate enterprise, full of humour, is soon superseded by Don John's far more sinister plot, and Don Pedro now unwittingly relinquishes the role of director for that of victim. The effect of this transformation is to lend some credibility to Claudio's reversal of attitude, just as Benedick's collusion had given some plausibility to the notion that Don Pedro had been disloyal earlier. Each incident helps to reinforce the pervasive theme of the difficulty of 'knowing' others. Thus, from Act III, Scene 2 onwards, Don Pedro loses some of his earlier initiative, as the plot involving Benedick and Beatrice gradually becomes more heavily dependent upon the events involving Claudio and Hero. In his witty exchange with Benedick at the beginning of Act V, Scene 1, we are reminded of his former superiority, but because we know that he has unwittingly become a victim of the very same device that he has used to entrap Benedick and Beatrice—that of disguise and deception—we view his character now from an ironical standpoint. But having said that, Don Pedro cannot remain a victim for long; when he realises Benedick is 'in earnest' in his challenge to Claudio (V.1.187), he begins to suspect the extent to which he himself has been manipulated:

> But soft you, let me be; pluck up, my heart, and be sad. Did he not say my brother was fled? (V.1.196–7)

With Don John's plot exposed, Don Pedro's role is virtually complete, and he appears in the final scene of the play as an observer rather than as a manipulator. His expression of wonder at Hero's resurrection: 'The former Hero! Hero that is dead!' (V.4.65), is one which we all share, while the final union of Benedick and Beatrice reaffirms the positive nature of the intuitions with which he has been associated throughout the play. He is very much part of the corporate exposure of human fallibility, since he too can be fooled by the power of visual 'evidence' alone.

Don John

Although Don John is a relatively minor character, the role he fulfils is an important one in that he is the source of malevolence in the play. The animosity between him and his brother, Don Pedro, is twice hinted at: 'Let me bid you welcome, my lord, being reconciled to the Prince your brother' (I.1.145–6), and later Conrade alludes to it in his advice to Don John (I.3.19ff.). In a play in which characters appear to use language prodigally, Don John's stony silence marks him out as something of an exception: 'I thank you. I am not of many words, but I thank you' (I.1.148–9), although we quickly realise that this silence is a mark of discontent.

We do not know why Don John is malicious or discontented. Like all of Shakespeare's 'illegitimate' characters, he carries a grudge which admits of no rational explanation. Indeed, when Conrade urges him to 'hear reason' (I.3.5), he dismisses the advice out of hand as being wholly ineffectual: 'And when I have heard it, what blessing brings it?' (I.3.8). His commitment to villainy flies directly in the face of any normal desire to live harmoniously with others, and he flatly refuses to change his actions or his attitude.

> I had rather be a canker in a hedge than a rose in his grace, and it better fits my blood to be disdained of all than to fashion a carriage to rob love from any. In this, though I cannot be said to be a flattering honest man, it must not be denied but I am a plain-dealing villain. I am trusted with a muzzle and enfranchised with a clog; therefore I have decreed not to sing in my cage. If I had my mouth I would bite; if I had my liberty, I would do my liking. In the meantime, let me be that I am and seek not to alter me.   (I.3.25–34)

Don John's frankness is disarming, and his allegations that he has been deprived of his freedom arouses a glimmer of sympathy in us. In practical terms, however, his open commitment to villainy makes the task of ultimate detection possible; for example, Benedick guesses that the disgrace of Hero has its source in Don John, whose 'spirits' are known to 'toil in frame of villainies' (IV.1.186–7), while his confiding in Conrade and Borachio virtually guarantees that his plots will ultimately be revealed. To this extent Don John's villainy is less concentrated than that of his counterparts in the tragedies, rather he is bumbling by comparison, and hence presents a weaker threat to order and stability in the final analysis.

In certain respects Don John exemplifies the seamier side of experience, helping to validate in the minds of some of the other characters certain commonplace arguments about infidelity, disloyalty, and human malice, rather than seeking to transcend the severe limitations they impose. For example, when he hears of 'an intended marriage', he shows no feelings of joy, rather, he seeks the chance to practise his villainy:

> Will it serve for any model to build mischief on? What is he for a
> fool that betroths himself to unquietness? (I.3.42–4)

This opposition to marriage confirms his generally anti-social behaviour, but when he learns that it is Claudio who intends marriage, he reveals a more specific and personal motive for his malice: 'That young start-up hath all the glory of my overthrow; if I can cross him any way, I bless myself every way' (I.3.61–3). This is not exactly a cause of his malice, rather it is a validation of it, and there is a sense in which his 'malignity' is, like that of Iago in *Othello*, 'motiveless'. Don John is what he is, and the best we can do is to acknowledge the existence of the force he represents. Shakespeare seeks to personalise this force, and the provision of specific motives is designed to disguise the fact that Don John represents a stubborn obstacle to the happiness of others.

The failure of Don John's first plot exposes nevertheless the vulnerability of others, but it also increases his desperate desire to do evil: 'Only to despite them I will endeavour anything' (II.1.29). This exaggerated posture is potentially dangerous, although events never allow us to take it too seriously. But he does bring out the worst in others, a fact amply demonstrated by Borachio's providing the suggestion for the second plot; when he asks: 'How canst thou cross this marriage?' he is told 'Not honestly, my lord; but so covertly that no dishonesty shall appear in me' (II.1.7–9). Moreover, so adept is he at manipulating others that he can be present himself at the scenario provided by Borachio (III.3.146–7), and he is also present for the public humiliation of Hero, lending his support to Claudio's allegations: 'Sir they are spoken, and these things are true' (IV.1.65). Although his deceptions are similar in principle to those of Don Pedro, it is clear that their respective intentions occupy opposite ends of the moral and social spectrum.

As with so many of Shakespeare's 'villains' Don John is successful only so long as his plots are not fully exposed to public view. The public confrontation between Claudio and Don Pedro and the latter's handing over of Hero (II.1.) effectively negate the allegation of disloyalty. But once both Claudio and Don Pedro are implicated as 'witnesses' of Hero's apparent infidelity, then the plot is given far more powerful credibility than it would otherwise possess. Too many of the other characters have seen someone whom they are led to believe is Hero, engaging in an act of infidelity, and moreover she cannot prove her innocence in the same way that Don Pedro had been able to demonstrate his loyalty. To this extent, Don John exposes Messina for the vulnerable society that it is, by encouraging the violation of trust in others, and this is his primary function in the play.

Leonato

Leonato is Hero's father, but he is also the Governor of Messina, responsible for law and order, and the dispensing of justice. He is a conventional father-figure in that he is concerned for his daughter's future, and he seeks to make careful provision for her happiness. For example, he refuses to accept uncritically Antonio's garbled story of Don Pedro's allegedly amorous intentions towards Hero, although he makes certain that she is well prepared for any advance which might be made to her:

> No, no; we will hold it as a dream, till it appear itself; but I will acquaint my daughter withal, that she be the better prepared for an answer, if peradventure this be true. (I.2.18–21)

He has, we know, already made lavish preparations for the entertainment of Don Pedro, to the extent that the latter actually comments upon his unusual generosity: 'The fashion of the world is to avoid cost, and you encounter it' (I.1.90–1). As the one character who is already married when the play begins, he seems aware of just how precarious human relationships can be, and yet his attitude is a positive one in that he generously acquiesces in the plot to bring Benedick and Beatrice together: 'My lord, I am for you, though it cost me ten nights' watching' (II.1.313–14).

But Leonato is also a man of the world, and this emerges in his conversations with Benedick and Beatrice. He rebukes Benedick with a gentle firmness when the latter jokes audaciously about Hero's parentage, rejecting out of hand this light-hearted imputation of mistrust of his own wife: 'Signior Benedick, no; for then were you a child' (I.1.100). Also, he recognises Beatrice's shrewdness in her dealings with others (II.1.71), although hers is not an independence of mind that he is prepared to accept in his own daughter: 'Daughter, remember what I told you. If the Prince do solicit you in that kind, you know your answer' (II.1.58–60). Thus, our early impressions of Leonato are those of a benign, generous, but careful father, trusting in his attitude towards others, and tolerant, but not naive.

However, like all those who confidently participate in the plot to deceive Benedick and Beatrice, he too becomes a victim of the more sinister deceptions of Don John. His circumstances are more acutely ironical than those of the others since from Act III, Scene 5 onwards he has it in his power as dispenser of justice, to expose and prevent the plot leading to his daughter's public disgrace. But ironically, in preparing vigorously for her wedding: 'Brief, I pray you, for you see it is a busy time with me' (III.5.4), he is helping to hasten Hero's downfall, since Dogberry and Verges, for all their tediousness are in possession of the very facts that will expose Don John's plot.

Leonato's careful preparations on one front leave him totally unprepared for Claudio's allegations against Hero on another. Consequently, he has no time to be sceptical, or indeed, to call for proof of their validity, and so he believes them. While Hero lies in a dead faint Leonato becomes the aggrieved father, feeling deeply the extent to which he is now publicly dishonoured by the activities of his own child, and responding quite irrationally to the situation:

> Could she here deny
> The story that is printed in her blood?
> Do not live, Hero, do not ope thine eyes;
> For, did I think thou wouldst not quickly die,
> Thought I thy spirits were stronger than thy shames,
> Myself would, on the rearward of reproaches,
> Strike at thy life. Grieved I. I had but one?
> Chid I for that at frugal Nature's frame?
> O, one too much by thee!
>
> (IV.1.119–27)

Of course, Leonato is not the only one to have been fooled; Claudio and Don Pedro also believe that Hero has been unfaithful, and this adds considerable weight to the allegations. Thus, while we may feel that his reactions are extreme, they do not alienate him entirely from our sympathies.

From Act IV, Scene 1 onwards, Leonato's grief overthrows many of the earlier impressions we have of his character. Antonio tries to comfort him, but his counsel is rejected:

> 'tis all men's office to speak patience
> To those that wring under the load of sorrow,
> But no man's virtue or sufficiency
> To be so moral when he shall endure
> The like himself.
>
> (V.1.27–31)

In a play in which we have come to expect reversals of attitude from nearly all of the characters, Leonato's speech prepares the ground for Antonio's swift transformation to irrational revenger later in the scene. Leonato's strength of feeling is one thing, but, of course, Hero is still alive, and he is party to the plan to test the validity of Claudio's allegations and his affections for Hero. Consequently, we are given no more than an impression of Leonato's sorrow, as the action moves swiftly on to his confrontation with Claudio. Where earlier our sympathies, though carefully controlled, were clear, they now become somewhat ambivalent. Is Leonato wholly serious in wanting to challenge Claudio for having 'killed' his daughter, or is he simply improvising upon Friar Francis's basic plan? His is the first of three challenges which follow in quick succession, so its force is dissipated in the comparisons and contrasts which follow, and yet it is difficult to appreciate clearly the tone of what Leonato says here. The consequences of his irrational behaviour seem ludicrous in that they deprive him of his sense of proportion, but he is quickly brought up short when he sees in the irrational behaviour of a suddenly transformed Antonio, a mirror image of his own irrationality, thus softening our response to his own grief in the light of a momentary comic effect.

In Act V, Scene 1, when Leonato learns the truth from Borachio, he resumes his former control, and sets about manipulating Claudio and Don Pedro with the kind of care that had characterised his earlier dealings with them. Thus, by the final scene of the play he regains his former composure in the confidence that this time his preparations will not prove fruitless. Although Leonato's dramatic function in the play is as an agency of plot, Shakespeare adds a measure of complexity to his character, making his reactions individual. His parental concern is harmonised with his wider commitment to social harmony, and although he never acknowledges his errors in the way that, say, Claudio does, he is prepared to help in any way he can to restore things to their former equilibrium.

Antonio

Although Antonio appears in only two scenes in the play (I.2 and V.1), he provides us with a clear example of the way in which Shakespeare often humanises minor characters whose primary function is to illuminate facets of plot.

Antonio is an 'old man' and this lends some plausibility to the inaccuracy of the story that he carries to Leonato early in the play. Antonio's report represents the first of a number of overheard conversations, and although it is not contrived like some of the others, it does garble the truth. Clearly, from the outset, age and experience seem to provide no certain proof against misunderstanding, and moreover, despite the superficial attractiveness of his story, there is no guarantee that it will be true. Antonio is not without caution, but his enthusiasm suggests that he would almost like the news he brings to be true:

As the event stamps them; but they have a good cover, they show well outward. (I.2.6–7)

If this is how the news appears from its outward manifestation, then we are given double proof of the hazards of judging by 'appearances', and we are made even more suspicious when Antonio characterises the servant from whom he got the story about Don Pedro's amorous intentions as 'A good sharp fellow' (I.2.16). For the moment, Antonio's gullibility can be attributed to his old age, but when we hear in the following scene (I.3) of the plot to pervert the course of the marriage between Claudio and Hero, then we realise that his credulousness is by no means an isolated phenomenon. Rather, he becomes for a moment the dramatic focus of a much deeper uncertainty which permeates the society of Messina generally.

When Antonio next appears, in Act V, Scene 1, it is again with Leonato, and again his behaviour provides a contrast with that of his brother. From being a carrier of inaccurate news to a more cautiously sceptical brother, he is now characterised as a 'reasonable' man, whose own rational grasp of 'wisdom' contrasts with Leonato's uncontrollable grief. He emphasises the essential childishness of Leonato's behaviour: 'Therein do men from children nothing differ' (V.1.33), but we become sceptical ourselves when we see the conclusion towards which his rational arguments tend:

Yet bend not all the harm upon yourself;
Make those that offend you suffer too.

(V.1.39–40)

In counselling personal 'revenge' Antonio is unwittingly perverting Justice itself (whose representative is, after all, Leonato), but the irony is compounded when his brother recognises this as 'reasonable' advice: 'There thou speak'st reason' (V.1.41). Antonio's 'reason' leads ultimately to the irrationality of 'revenge', and Shakespeare takes care to expose the emptiness of his advice prior to his change of behaviour when he confronts Claudio later in the scene. Antonio's reversal of attitude is, thus, more than simply an attempt to achieve a momentary comic effect. On the contrary it is shown to be rooted in his character, and can be compared to what we saw of his earlier appearance, in that he becomes the focus for a number of ideas that the play has been concerned to develop. Leonato is understandably shocked by the sudden impassioned speech of his brother, and his futile attempts to interrupt divert our attention to the intrinsic comedy of the situation. But

Antonio's insults reflect upon what he has already said to Leonato by way of advice, and they also echo Beatrice's earlier objections (IV.1) to male deceit:

> *What, man! I know them, yea,*
> *And what they weigh, even to the utmost scruple—*
> *Scambling, out-facing, fashion-monging boys,*
> *That lie and cog and flout, deprave and slander,*
> *Go anticly, show outward hideousness,*
> *And speak off half a dozen dangerous words,*
> *How they might hurt their enemies, if they durst;*
> *And this is all.*
>
> (V.1.92–9)

Ironically, these accusations, though they have some general application, are quite misplaced since both Claudio and Don Pedro have already proved that they are not without honour. But they do pave the way for Benedick's challenge which follows, in that these are the very allegations that he has been called upon by Beatrice to disprove. Finally, although Antonio's apparent confusion here seems well in character, his outburst draws attention away from Leonato, who up to this point has been the centre of attention in this scene. The latter is quite suddenly, and surprisingly, relegated to the role of spectator, and this transformation lightens considerably the mood of this potentially dangerous encounter.

Dogberry

Dogberry is another of the play's 'minor' characters whose primary function is to advance the plot, but Shakespeare individualises him with considerable success. When he first appears in Act III, Scene 3 he is instructing the Watch in their duties. From the outset Dogberry divorces words from their meanings in that he almost always expresses the exact opposite of what he intends: 'First, who think you the most desartless man to be constable?' (III.3.9–10). This becomes an identifiable character trait, but his mangling of language also reflects one of the play's major themes, in that, just as his words are divorced from his thoughts, and hence have the capacity to confuse or even deceive the listener, so he exemplifies the comic possibilities of the discrepancy between language, thought, and action, which informs the two parallel plots in the play. In Dogberry and his colleagues language is reduced to a series of all but meaningless counters which simply fail to reflect thought either accurately or adequately. But even so, Dogberry never means to engage in any wilful act of deceit or confusion; rather his use of language is symptomatic of the larger problem with which the play is concerned.

Dogberry is an authoritarian character, even though he lacks the ability to make himself clearly understood. From the beginning he is prone to the kind of digression that exposes his own sense of self-importance, and he has occasionally to be prompted by his colleague Verges, who is invariably far more direct than he is: 'Well, give them their charge, neighbour Dogberry' (III.3.8). And yet it is in the hands of the Constable and his Watch that the safety of the inhabitants of Messina rests. If Leonato's capacity for being deceived gives us little confidence in the rational process of Law in Messina, then, surely, we have even greater qualms when we consider the responsibility and the limited ability of the Watch.

For all his apparent incompetence, Dogberry is not without humanity. In his own curious way he is aware of the extent to which 'evil' can pervert those it touches, but on the other hand, he is reluctant to be too harsh on anyone who shows evidence of possessing the slightest grain of honesty: 'Truly, I would not hang a dog by my will, much more a man who hath any honesty in him' (III.3.61–2). Also, in a curious way, Dogberry presides over an act of 'impersonation', since the Watch is called upon to 'represent' the person of the Prince, and hence his Law: 'This is the end of the charge: you, constable, are to present the Prince's own person; if you meet the Prince in the night, you may stay him'(III.3.72–4). Of course, Dogberry doesn't know what 'impersonation' involves, but he strays ignorantly into an area which connects his advice with some of the play's larger concerns, and links his instruction with Don John's wilful mistaking of Claudio (II.1.146), the deception of Benedick (II.3) and Beatrice (III.1), and Borachio and Margaret's impersonations.

It is, of course, ironic that Dogberry and his colleagues should be in possession of the facts concerning the plot to disgrace Hero, but that their tedious linguistic diversions should prove the barrier to immediate revelation. Dogberry's overweening self-esteem (combined with a perverse generosity) contrives to prevent him from revealing all to Leonato in Act III, Scene 5. Indeed, when Verges speaks directly to the Governor, he is patronisingly dismissed by Dogberry as worthy but inferior, although we are sharply aware that in this case the commonplace wisdom he draws upon to support his contention is inapposite:

A good old man, sir, he will be talking; as they say, 'When the age is in, the wit is out'. God help us, it is a world to see! Well said, i' faith neighbour Verges; well, God's a good man; an two men ride of a horse, one must ride behind. (III.5.32–36)

Leonato, however, believing that Dogberry does not have anything important to tell him, asks him to examine the prisoners himself, thereby ensuring the protraction of the proceedings, and hastening the downfall of his own daughter. Dogberry's bumbling incompetence provides just the right kind of psychological justification for withholding the information about Borachio's plot, and hence disguises the dramatist's manipulation of character according to the dictates of dramatic design. Indeed, Dogberry is so concerned with himself that when he comes to examine the two felons he responds to Conrade's calling him 'ass' and 'coxcombe' with such vehemence that he relinquishes the necessary disinterest demanded of him as a judge. So personally affronted is he by these insults that he is prompted to recount after his own fashion his own personal qualities:

> I am a wise fellow, and, which is more, an officer; and, which is more, a householder; and, which is more, as pretty a piece of flesh as any in Messina; and one that knows the law, go to; and a rich fellow enough, go to; and a fellow that hath had losses; and one that hath two gowns and everything handsome about him. Bring him away. O that I had been writ down an ass! (IV.2.77–84)

Our interest in characters such as Dogberry in the play is generated specifically in order to divert our attention from the potential seriousness of other issues. Moreover, although the Watch appears only four times between Acts III and V (III.3, III.5, IV.2, and V.1), Shakespeare manages in his drawing of the character of Dogberry to provide a remarkable psychological fullness for him which makes his every action seem natural. The incomprehensibility recognized by Don Pedro at the end of the play has a justification from within the character: 'This learned Constable is too cunning to be understood' (V.1.217–18), but it is he and his colleagues whose 'shallowness' defeats the 'wisdom' of the other characters in the play; to this extent Borachio's observation is correct:

> I have deceived even your very eyes: what your wisdoms could not discover, these shallow fools have brought to light. (V.1.220–2)

Friar Francis

Friar Francis appears in only two scenes (IV.1 and V.4) and is, in some ways, the most sketchily drawn of all the characters in the play. But like Margaret, and, to a lesser extent, Conrade and Borachio, his function is to focus attention on a number of issues with which the central action is concerned. Unlike Leonato or Antonio, who are 'experienced' but susceptible to deception and the pressures of the moment, Friar Francis weighs evidence carefully before passing judgement. In a technical sense Shakespeare requires an agent to carry the plot forward after the disgrace of Hero, but it has to harmonise with what went before. Thus, in the wider context of the practice of 'observing' and 'noting', what Friar Francis says in response to Hero's gestures of shock and dismay provides a thoughtful, but not uncharacteristic counterbalance to Leonato's hasty acquiescence in Claudio's story.

While others speak he remains silent, wrapped in contemplation, so that when he does divulge his opinion, he sees well beyond the pressures of the particular situation:

> Call me a fool,
> Trust not my reading nor my observations,
> Which with experimental seal doth warrant
> The tenor of my book; trust not my age,
> My reverence, calling, nor divinity,
> If this sweet lady lie not guiltless here
> Under some biting error.
>
> (IV.1.162–8)

Friar Francis focuses for us the notion of the sanctity of marriage, and its ultimate functioning as a means whereby society regenerates itself. Hence, his plot, which is a similar one (in intention at any rate) to that designed to bring Benedick and Beatrice together, has a positive value in the play, and directs us towards a conclusion which is both festive and religious. As a contemplative man, Friar Francis has observed humanity, and has learned to 'read' human behaviour accurately. In Act IV, Scene 1 our sympathies are clearly with his analysis since we know that he is substantially correct, so that although he is a 'mouthpiece' for certain pervasive ideas, they emanate naturally from his character.

There is a sense in which, despite his minimal contribution to the final scene of the play, the Friar's role is analogous to that of the dramatist himself. As a religious character he knows all, and as a participant in the play he is in full possession of all the details of the plan to ressurect Hero:

> All this amazement I can qualify,
> When, after that the holy rites are ended,
> I'll tell you largely of fair Hero's death,
> Meantime let wonder seem familiar,
> And to the chapel let us presently.
>
> (V.4.67–71)

And yet, of course, the organisation of the plot is ultimately attributable to Shakespeare the dramatist. The Friar, therefore, exemplifies the technique whereby the dramatist's hand in the plot is concealed by placing the onus upon a character who is plausible enough to carry the burden without straining credibility. In placing it in the hands of Friar Francis, Shakespeare creates a character whose own experience and contemplative skills are believable, and who can bestow upon the plot a religious importance which reflects the 'fortunate' workings of Providence itself.

The language of *Much Ado About Nothing*

The Elizabethan stage contained no scenery, and so the burden of expounding the action rested firmly upon the dramatist's and the actors' combined powers to evoke a sense of place, and atmosphere, through language. *Much Ado About Nothing* employs these resources to the full, both at a thematic level (as the Benedick–Beatrice plot illustrates) and at a more fundamental technical level. The language of the play falls conveniently into two categories, the one formal, poetic, and 'literary'—exemplifying the 'romantic' inclinations of characters such as Claudio, and Hero, but extending to include Leonato and Antonio, and, in one important context, Benedick and Beatrice—and the other, natural, more 'realistic' in its unpredictable flexibility, and not far removed from the rhythms of everyday speech.

When employing verse dialogue, the basic metre which Shakespeare uses is the iambic pentameter, a combination of five strong and five weakly stressed syllables distributed alternately throughout a single line. But as his own style developed the metrical patterns of his blank verse became more flexible, able to cope with more complex expressions of intense emotion, while his own prose became even more rich and rhythmically varied. In *Much Ado About Nothing* the lofty artificiality of poetic expression is often undercut by the 'realism' of prose dialogue, and each is made to provide a comment on the other as modes of more or less adequate expression. For example, Claudio's revelation of his love for Hero is expressed in a stiff and formal blank verse which contrasts vividly with the varied rhythms of the prose dialogues which precede it:

> When you went onward on this ended action
>
> I looked upon her with a soldier's eye,
>
> That liked but had a rougher task in hand
>
> Than to drive liking to the name of love;
>
> But now I am returned and that war-thoughts
>
> Have left their places vacant, in their rooms
>
> Come thronging soft and delicate desires,
>
> All prompting me how fair young Hero is,
>
> Saying I liked her ere I went to wars. (I.1.276–84)

Here the clumsy opening line with its extra syllable gives way to a measured utterance which seems too distant and insipid to carry much conviction, and which speaks of the seemingly mechanical replacement of one set of thoughts by another. The military man has now become transformed into a conventional lover, but as the action develops we learn to suspect such transformations. Don Pedro, whose manner is formal but whose utterance is made to carry much more conviction, makes this very point in his reply, and opens up for us the whole question of expression and its thematic significance:

> *Thou wilt be like a lover presently*
> *And tire the hearer with a book of words.*
> (I.1.85-6)

Throughout the play, both Claudio and Hero are 'acted upon' by others, although they themselves do participate in the plot to deceive Benedick and Beatrice. Moreover, although they are not conscious of the postures which they strike, we are made to perceive the sheer inflexibility of their responses. Claudio fails to perceive the truth as distinct from the perversions of it to which he falls victim, while even Hero (for whose plight we have much more sympathy) seems reluctant to engage in the frank communication of the truths of experience, even when Margaret confronts her with one of them (see III.4.22ff.)

Claudio's preoccupation with the formal expression of his love for Hero has one further important consequence. If, as we suggested, his words seem to carry less than full conviction, then we are prevented from sympathising for any length of time with his predicament; indeed, his feelings remain distant from us. This question of 'distance' is crucial to our understanding of the larger dramatic technique which Shakespeare employs thoroughly throughout the play, and it serves the function of holding in check potentially devasting forces which could precipitate tragedy. But the establishment of a standard of formal 'literary' expression also lays the foundation for comedy later in the play. For example, after hearing a catalogue of his faults which force him to change his attitude towards Beatrice, Benedick addresses her when she enters in a blank verse which contrasts starkly with the devasting force of her own sinewy, prosaic utterance:

> BENEDICK: Fair Beatrice, I thank you for your pains.
> BEATRICE: I took no more pains for those thanks than you take pains
> to thank me; if it had been painful, I would not have come.
> (II.3.41–4)

We know, of course, that Beatrice did not come to call Benedick because she had any affection for him, a factor which makes their talking at cross purposes funny. As for Beatrice, she is as a consequence of her ignorance of the circumstances of Benedick's transformation, able to dismantle his poetic utterance by recasting in literal prose the very words he has used. The deflationary effect which this juxtaposition of two kinds of language produces simply intensifies the comic nature of this encounter. As we learn later, however, neither Benedick nor Beatrice are at ease in expressing themselves in the conventional literary language of romantic lovers—their 'halting' sonnets show this at the end of the play—but their various encounters, which become in certain respects conflicts between styles of utterance, serve to penetrate the linguistic postures naively maintained by Hero and Claudio. In this design the language of the Watch proves to be a kind of prose which is so flexible that it takes no account of meaning whatever, but apart from its obviously comic function, it assists in the process of isolating 'words' as an unreliable index of human thought, feeling and intention. Thus each style of expression in the play represents some form of distortion, and the interplay between them culminates in a profound statement about the function of language itself.

Scenes and structure

Our concern with characterisation and language has really been a concern with some of the fundamental details of dramatic structure. Another basic unit of structure is the 'scene', since it is through the careful positioning of individual scenes in the play that a pattern of meaning emerges. Scenes are usually separated from each other by distinct pauses as one group of characters leaves the stage and is replaced by another. An obvious example occurs at the end of Act I, Scene 1 when the stage is cleared, indicating both a lapse of time and a change of place for Act I, Scene 2. This pause, following immediately upon the formulation of the Claudio–Don Pedro plot to secure Hero, is dramatically necessary since it initiates the first of a series of misunderstandings which will have far-reaching consequences for nearly all of the characters in the play. As audience, we 'overhear' correctly the details of Don Pedro's plan (as we do elsewhere in the play with all the other plots), but we also get the opportunity to observe the extent to which 'overhearing', as a means of gathering information, carries with it certain risks. The situation is further complicated as we are asked to distinguish between Antonio's reporting of what is an accidental mistake, which is answered by a cautious response from Leonato, and Don John's engineering of error in the scene which follows (I.3), which is deliberately designed to deceive others and to cause mischief. This rapid succession of scenes serves to introduce some of the various perspectives that one issue—that of mistaking the truth—can sustain.

We do notice also in the play that certain changes of focus (not place, or time) occur within individual scenes, rather similar to the way in which a film camera focuses now on one object, then on another. There is, of course, the case of the Dogberry scenes which progress alongside those involving the other characters, and which are clearly not fully synchronised with the main action until the very end, and this change of focus is very significant. But in addition to these, there are units of design within particular scenes (we could perhaps call these 'episodes'), through which certain important juxtapositions of both characters and ideas are executed. For example, in Act I, Scene 1, attention shifts from the initial 'ensemble' or group episode of the welcoming of the Messenger (I.1.1–29), to a more specific dialogue between Beatrice and the Messenger (I.1.30–88) which establishes the existence of a 'merry war' between her and Benedick, and thence to another group episode as Don Pedro and his entourage enter. The focus continually alternates between these large group dialogues, and other more intimate encounters, and the ideas and attitudes which emerge supplement each other in the various contexts in which they are made to appear. In this way a texture of extraordinary richness is created.

This technique of juxtaposing scenes and dialogues is used frequently throughout *Much Ado About Nothing*, and, indeed, may be found in all of Shakespeare's plays. But the ordering of scenes and incidents fulfils an added function in this play since it becomes the primary means whereby its comic tone is ultimately preserved. From the very outset we observe how one episode or scene is made to comment on another, and we follow through the various plots to their fruition. For example, the resolution of the Claudio–Don Pedro plot initiated in Act I, Scene 1, and culminating in a satisfactory conclusion in Act II, Scene 1 (and which is, in relation to the main plot of the play, a kind of false start) provides the occasion for the initiation of the parallel Beatrice–Benedick plot, but this second plot is quickly capped by another in Act II, Scene 3 which is designed to convert Claudio and Don Pedro from the roles of manipulators to those of victims using precisely the same means that they intend to employ against Benedick and Beatrice. In this way a pattern of ironies is built up whereby we are able, from a superior position of knowledge, to judge the actions and attitudes of each set of characters as they proceed in partial ignorance of the consequences of their actions.

The positive intention of the Don Pedro–Claudio plot (II.1) is balanced by the destructive potential of the Don John plot; the 'legitimate' brother acts for good, while the 'illegitimate' brother can only do evil. Or to put it another way, the one plot seeks to negate any pleasure which we might derive from the other. But, in the essentially comic world of the play, Don John's plot cannot be allowed complete success since this would result in a cynical distortion of some vital aspects of experience itself. The action acknowledges the existence of evil as an element of human experience but it also reinforces the view that evil can only dominate in an atmosphere of total ignorance. Thus, the plot to pervert the relationship between Hero and Claudio is always followed by scenes which emphasise more positive issues, and these are dwelt on at much greater length; thus, Act II, Scene 2, which is a mere 51 lines long, is quickly followed by the more positive events of Act II, Scene 3 which is 255 lines long. Moreover, whereas in Act II, Scene 3 and Act III Scene 1 we actually overhear the deception of Benedick and Beatrice respectively, the second deception of Claudio and Don Pedro is simply reported (III.3.149ff.). Moreover, the twisting of the Claudio–Hero relationship is not initiated until *after* both Benedick and Beatrice have resolved to change their attitudes toward each other, so that we see both the happy occasion, and its obverse: 'O day untowardly turned!' (III.2.119). But even here, we are not allowed to ponder the implications of this reversal. Our attention moves swiftly to a new set of characters who now take the stage, Dogberry and the Watch (III.2), and it is their comic antics which help to hold in check our contemplation of the serious issue which has recently been revealed, but whose arrival we had been expecting for some time. Moreover, although the plot laid by Don John has yet to be carried out by Borachio, it comes to light through 'overhearing', thereby introducing a new tension, which requires the synchronisation of the activities of Dogberry and his colleagues with those of Leonato and his family before a happy conclusion can be reached. In this way, the obstacle to a happy conclusion is as much the ponderousness of Dogberry and his colleagues as it is the evil intentions of Don John, thus depriving the evil which the latter represents of its potential for irreversible destruction. This alternation between seriousness and levity permeates the entire play, and is even present in the most extended serious scene, that involving the rejection of Hero at Act IV, Scene 1. Here Claudio's potentially tragic mistake is capable of being 'turned' thanks to the experienced observation and ingenuity of Friar Francis who initiates a plot which will bring about the happy ending which the comedy requires in order to restore its tonal balance. Moreover, as if this plot were not sufficient, the dialogue between Beatrice and Benedick which closes the scene offers us a foretaste with its mixture of seriousness and levity.

By the end of Act IV this alternation of moods has virtually become a principle of the play's dramatic design, controlling our distance from the characters themselves, and the actions in which they are involved. Thus, by the time we reach Act V, Scene 1 we are able to cope with the rapid sequence of reversals which take place in this scene as 'reason' is supplanted by inexplicable irrationality, and as self-indulgence gives way to opposition of a more principled nature. In this way our sympathies are controlled, extended to particular characters for short spaces of time, and then withdrawn, and each episode draws from us a surprising complexity of response. Throughout the play, and particularly in Act V, Scene 1, characters are constantly brought to the point of serious confrontation, and with one notable (though ultimately reparable) exception, are made to withdraw before any lasting harm is done. Here the theme of language as a substitute for action is carefully harmonised with plot and scenic structure, revealing the extent to which a remarkably close control is exerted on the action.

These are only a few of the many examples in the play of the positioning of scenes and incidents which serve to enrich the dramatic action. In each case we should observe the characters involved, and also the context in which these incidents take place. This web of incident and character makes the structure of the play complex and compact.

Part 4

Hints for study

WHEN READING a play we should always guard against the temptation to treat it as though it were a novel. This is often a difficult point to grasp, but we must always bear in mind that a play is designed primarily to be performed, usually in a particular type of building, a theatre, rather than to be read privately. The novelist's medium is solely the words on the page, and what they contain in the way of meaning gives us the information we require to judge the actions and behaviour of each character. The novelist is also in complete control of the pace at which the story unfolds, just as the reader, for his part, is able to control the speed at which he reads it.

But in a play the kind of detailed description of the lives, relationships, and situations of particular characters that we expect from a novel is absent, partly because the sheer pressure of performance in a particular place at a particular time makes their inclusion impossible. Also, because his words are designed to be spoken by actors, the dramatist cannot halt the flow of his play, just as members of the theatre audience cannot ask that the action be stopped for a moment to allow individuals to ponder particular details. In a play the dramatist can only work through the mouths of his characters, unlike the novelist who can adopt a series of different narrative postures. The action of a play is embodied in the characters who present it.

We should always remember that in a dialogue in a play our attention is not engaged solely by what the speaker is saying, but also by the actions and responses of the character who is listening. On the printed page a dramatic dialogue seems incomplete. Only in performance does it achieve fullness. Here the physical characteristics of speaker and listener, tones of voice, movements, gestures, and facial expressions all contribute to the play's meaning. Consider, for example, Claudio's silence at II.1.269ff. It is a silence which, as Beatrice points out, betokens jealousy since he thinks that Don Pedro has stolen Hero from him. Here his feelings are expressed not in words, but in gestures, but this gives way to another kind of silence when he realises that he has been wrong, and is urged to speak:

Silence is the perfectest herald of joy; I were but little happy, if I could say how much. Lady, as you are mine, I am yours; I give away myself for you and dote upon the exchange. (II.1.282–5)

Moreover, much later in the play, at Act V, Scene 1 when Claudio learns the truth about how Borachio had deceived him into thinking Hero unfaithful, he remains silent throughout, although we must not assume that he is not reacting to the news. Indeed, when he does finally speak, it is to describe his non-verbal responses: 'I have drunk poison whiles he uttered it.' (V.1.233). In a play which makes much of the opposition between 'words' and 'actions' and between language and silence, it is necessary to visualise the dramatic action. When we read the play we are required to infer information about the visual aspects of performance, and throughout we are asked to observe the discrepancies between what characters say and do, and between what they see and hear. All this is part of the adjustment of imaginative perception that we need to make in order to understand fully the text of a play. We must always remember that what we read in the study is really a design intended for performance, and not a substitute for it.

Essay questions and revision

(1) How relevant is the title of *Much Ado About Nothing* to the action of the play?

(2) Write an essay on Shakespeare's handling of the plot in *Much Ado About Nothing*.

(3) Show how Shakespeare harmonises plot and character in *Much Ado About Nothing*.

(4) Show how Shakespeare controls the conflict between 'good' and 'evil' in *Much Ado About Nothing*.

(5) What do the Dogberry scenes contribute to the overall design of *Much Ado About Nothing*?

(6) What is the significance of the Beatrice–Benedick conflict in *Much Ado About Nothing*?

(7) Analyse and comment upon the wit-combats in which Beatrice and Benedick engage in *Much Ado About Nothing* showing what they contribute to the development of the play's themes.

(8) Analyse critically the attitudes advanced in the play towards marriage, and the relationships between men and women.

(9) Write an essay on Shakespeare's use of comic irony in *Much Ado About Nothing*.

(10) Show how Shakespeare controls the threat to the comic tone of the play presented by Don John.

(11) Analyse the various ways in which Shakespeare controls our response to character and situation in *Much Ado About Nothing*.

(12) Compare and contrast the attitudes towards human relationships revealed in the Beatrice–Benedick conflict with that of the Claudio–Hero relationship in *Much Ado About Nothing*.

(13) Comment on the various ways in which Shakespeare employs the device of 'overhearing' in *Much Ado About Nothing*.

(14) What steps does Shakespeare take to preserve the comic tone of *Much Ado About Nothing*? Give specific examples and comment upon them.

(15) In the comic society of Messina the Law is an ass. If this is so, then how is a satisfactory conclusion to the action brought about in *Much Ado About Nothing*?

(16) Write notes on any TWO of the following characters in *Much Ado About Nothing*, and show the various ways in which they contribute to the dramatic action of the play: Margaret, Don Pedro, Antonio, Leonato, Claudio, Hero, Balthazar, Friar Francis, Borachio.

(17) Write an essay on language in *Much Ado About Nothing* showing both its particular uses, and what it contributes to the play's thematic development.

(18) How does Shakespeare manage to maintain the balance between seriousness and lightheartedness in *Much Ado About Nothing*?

(19) Write an essay on the theme of deception in *Much Ado About Nothing*.

(20) 'Man is a giddy thing, and that is my conclusion.' Explain what Benedick means by this, and consider to what extent *Much Ado About Nothing* is about the contradictions in human nature.

Answering questions

When answering essay questions, you should first read the question *carefully*. Once you are sure you understand it, you should then spend a little time (perhaps about five minutes) planning your answer. Because you will be expected to *explain* your response to the question, you will, therefore, wish to advance your strongest arguments, and the ordering of your ideas and the selection of suitable quotations will help you to do this.

When you are ready to write, introduce your discussion with a short paragraph explaining what you intend to do in your answer. Then lead into your first point. You should have time to make six or seven points in any one answer. If you build your argument in this way, taking a separate paragraph for each major point you have to make, and following through in each case with a detailed examination of your illustrations, then you will have no difficulty in convincing a reader that your argument is a valid one. This procedure has the added advantage of forcing you to think your ideas through, so that you can recognise difficulties for yourself, and overcome them. This is also a useful way of learning to *apply* your knowledge of a play like *Much Ado About Nothing*. Remember that the secret of thorough study is to work your way through a play anticipating the questions which it raises. In this way you can solve most of the difficulties it poses before you answer questions in an examination.

Here are two answers which have been sketched out, and which are designed to help you organise your own responses to the play.

Show how Shakespeare harmonises plot and character in
Much Ado About Nothing

---

1. This is a question about the extent to which characters are manipulated in accordance with the larger demands of the comic plot. Are Shakespeare's characters simply pawns, to be moved about at whim by the dramatist? Or is some attempt made to humanise them so that the plots in which they are involved have some basis in their own characters? It is not sufficient simply to relate the events of the plot in a question of this kind.

2. The obvious character to begin with is Don John, since we may object to his existence in the play simply as an agent of 'evil', an obstacle required to be overcome by the lovers before a happy ending can be achieved. His motive is clear (see I.3.60ff.) although in any case he is the 'bastard' brother of Don Pedro, and as such can be expected to engage in activities designed to disrupt the harmony of the play. Thus, although he is an evil figure, a kind of 'type' character, some plausible motives are ascribed to him, and they have the effect of diverting our attention slightly from the function he fulfils in the plot. In this case deception becomes a logical activity for one so evil to engage in, and we are therefore not surprised when he is involved in two plots to disrupt the Claudio–Hero relationship.

3. Don John is a character who *acts upon* others, and as such we might legitimately contrast him with characters like Claudio and Don Pedro, or even Friar Francis (though his case is slightly different as we shall see). They too contrive plots to change the circumstances of others, but their motive is different.

4. One issue raised by the Claudio–Don Pedro plot involves the extent to which Claudio becomes an unthinking puppet dancing to the tune which Don John plays. Can Claudio's reversals of attitude towards Hero be justified on psychological grounds, or is he made to change simply in order to fulfil the requirements of the comic plot? Although a full character-sketch of Claudio is not necessary here, his changeability might be observed (see I.1.275ff.), and his immaturity which reveals itself in his willingness to believe anything but the evidence of his own personal experience. But his suspicions are given some plausibility; for example, Benedick corroborates his first suspicion, and Don Pedro his second, so that what *is* clearly established is the uncertainty which

bedevils human relationships generally. It is this uncertainty which gives a larger plausibility to the reversals of plot.

5. The next set of characters to be considered are Beatrice and Benedick. Their initial hostility towards each other provides much of the early comic interest of the play, but we must ask ourselves how plausible their change of heart is. Their progress through the play is, therefore, one of learning, and our interest in the vicissitudes of their own psychological development allows us to accept, without too much irritation, their functions within the plot of the play.

6. Two other sets of characters remain to be considered: they are Dogberry and the Watch, and Friar Francis. Let us consider Dogberry and his colleagues first. It is their bumbling incompetence which prevents the Don John plot from coming to light too soon. Thus in some respects they share the burden of blame for the rejection of Hero, and hence lessen the force of the evil which Don John represents. Also, the information does not come to light quickly because Dogberry and his colleagues are too ponderous to do anything at speed. From Act III, Scene 2 onwards, the interest lies in exactly when these details will finally be synchronised, and the new tension which this creates and which has its source in Dogberry's absurd punctiliousness, effectively clothes the bare mechanics of the plot.

7. Finally, Friar Francis is entrusted with the plot which will finally resolve the dilemma of the lovers. But this is not just another plot involving deception. As a priest he lends dignity and sanctity to the enterprise, and fulfils the role of a kind of 'providence' within the play. His natural inclination to study and contemplation, and his accurate 'reading' of Hero's gestures allows us to accept naturally the deception which he engineers upon Claudio as being wholly for the good. Thus, the harmonious ending to the play emanates from within itself, and is not imposed perfunctorily upon the action from the outside. Throughout Shakespeare takes care to harmonise plot and character.

Write an essay on Shakespeare's use of comic irony in
Much Ado About Nothing

---

1. Shakespeare's use of irony in *Much Ado About Nothing* is extensive, involving situations, characters, and language itself. Irony arises from our awareness of the discrepancy between what the characters themselves believe is happening, and what they say in certain situations, and what we, as audience, actually know to be the case. In the play we are constantly being asked to equate our own superior knowledge of character and situation with that which the participants in the action possess themselves, and the comedy which emerges from our awareness of these discrepancies gives a measure of complexity to the dramatic design of

the play. The irony is comic because in the final analysis the conclusion of the action is a happy one, with the characters succeeding in overcoming the obstacles placed in their way.

2. Irony in the play is of three kinds, involving (a) character, (b) situation, and (c) language. A good example of Shakespeare's use of irony involving character might be the parallel changes of attitude which Beatrice and Benedick have towards each other. From the outset Beatrice is established as a 'realistic' character: 'I have a good eye, uncle; I can see a church by daylight' (II.1.72–3), and she is opposed to the notion of marriage since she believes (perhaps rather arrogantly) that no man is worthy of her. But for all this realism of outlook, and despite her alleged ability to 'apprehend' the motives of others, she is deceived in Act III, Scene 1 into believing that she has misjudged Benedick, and she resolves to change. From this point on she lays aside her 'wit' and struggles to find a language which will adequately describe her feelings, but the situation is exacerbated by her earlier railing against the very condition which she now espouses. Right to the end of the play she is forced to preserve a 'public' face, which reminds us of her earlier attitude, and she has to be trapped, like Benedick, into a sense of the contradictions in her own character. Thus what she *thinks* she knows about herself is clearly at odds with what at least some of the other characters know about her, and with what we know about all of them.

3. The case of Benedick is a little more complicated since by Act III, Scene 1 Hero and Ursula are in part correct in saying that he is in love with Beatrice. But in Act II, Scene 3 Benedick has no evidence whatever upon which to base his change of heart except the contrived dialogue which he has overheard. Indeed, this scene begins with his reiterating his rejection of marriage, although it does not take much to persuade him to change his mind. What he overhears leads him, so he thinks, to a new knowledge of himself, although we know that it is an awareness which has very little basis in reality. The irony of Benedick's position, and indeed, his character here, is that he is now doing exactly what Beatrice had earlier accused him of doing: changing his 'faith' according to each new 'fashion' (see I.1.69–71), and yet we know that there is more to genuine self-knowledge than that. Benedick has far further to go than he thinks, and it is the distance between *his* notion of himself and ours which provides the source for the comic irony attached to his character.

4. The play abounds with ironies of situation. Don Pedro's offer to woo Hero for Claudio provides one occasion, since it creates an ambiguous impression upon more than one character in the play. Also, the series of plots within plots, whereby manipulators are transformed into victims, all contribute to the kind of irony of situation which generates an

awareness in us of the disparity between the knowledge that the characters themselves possess concerning their predicaments, and that which, as omniscient observers, we ourselves know to be the case.

5. Perhaps the most amusing of the ironies which combine situation and character involves Dogberry and the Watch. Dogberry's knowledge of himself is flatly at odds with what we see of him, and yet, ironically, the information to which he unwittingly has access is crucial to the resolution of the play, and might, had it come to light earlier, have prevented Claudio from committing so serious an error of judgement. Indeed, it is this information which actually controls much of the situational irony in the latter part of the play, as characters like Leonato dismiss the Watch at the very time when they should have listened to their tedious expositions (see III.5.45–6).

6. From Act IV, Scene 1 onwards, and from the initiation of Friar Francis's plot, each occasion involving Leonato, Antonio, Claudio, and Don Pedro is fraught with irony. The potentially tragic irony of Hero's fate (her situation is, fortunately, reparable) gives way to a succession of 'mixed' situations as Claudio and Don Pedro are manipulated for different reasons, firstly by Leonato and Antonio, and secondly by Benedick. This culminates in Claudio's obsequies, performed at Act V, Scene 3, which finds a parallel in Beatrice's manipulation of Benedick. In the final two acts of the play the complexity of ironies is considerable.

7. Augmenting irony of character and situation, is the verbal irony which the play contains. Perhaps the best examples may be drawn from Beatrice's and Benedick's avowals that they will never marry, oaths and 'faiths' which they promptly break. But the position is complicated, since the superiority of the characters who deceive them both, simply serves to expose their own ignorance of human experience as they themselves fall prey to the same verbal deceptions that they perpetrate upon others. The result is one of a complex series of layers of irony, all neatly interwoven, exposing both the comic and the serious possibilities inherent in the actions, attitudes, and words, of the characters involved.

Part 5

Suggestions for further reading

The texts

Of the various texts available the following three are the most convenient modern editions, and of them, R.A. Foakes's edition is perhaps the most useful.

Much Ado About Nothing, ed. R.A. Foakes, Penguin Books, Harmondsworth, 1968.

Much Ado About Nothing, ed. D. Stevenson, Signet, New York, 1964.

Much Ado About Nothing, ed. J. Dover Wilson, Cambridge University Press, Cambridge, 1923.

Criticism

BRADBROOK, M.C.: *Shakespeare and Elizabethan Poetry*, Penguin Books, Harmondsworth, 1951. Concentrates on Claudio's self-deception.

BROWN, J.R.: *Shakespeare and His Comedies*, Methuen, London, 1957. Deals with the series of plays-within-plays in *Much Ado About Nothing*.

CRAIK, T.W.: '*Much Ado About Nothing*', *Scrutiny*, 19 (1952–3). A good scene-by-scene analysis of the play, much more favourably disposed to Claudio as a character than many other studies.

EVANS, BERTRAND: *Shakespeare's Comedies*, Oxford University Press, Oxford, 1960. Offers an unflattering view of Claudio.

JORGENSEN, P.A.: *Redeeming Shakespeare's Words*, California, 1962. Investigates the meanings of the word 'nothing' in the play.

LEGGATT, A.: *Shakespeare's Comedy of Love*, Methuen, London, 1974. Views the Claudio–Hero relationship as 'conventional', and the Beatrice–Benedick relationship as more natural.

MULRYNE, J.R.: *Much Ado About Nothing*, Studies in English Literature, no. 16, Edward Arnold, London, 1965. The most thorough treatment of the play both as a text for critical study, and as a play to be performed in the theatre.

ORMEROD, D.: 'Faith and Fashion in *Much Ado About Nothing*', *Shakespeare Survey*, 25, 1972. Looks at the oppositions between 'faith' and 'fashion', and 'appearance' and 'reality' in the play.

ROSSITER, A.P.: *Angel With Horns*, Longman, London, 1961. Deals with the various kinds of deception in the play.

The author of these notes

JOHN DRAKAKIS was educated at University College Cardiff, where he read English and History. He then obtained a Dip. Ed., at St Luke's College, Exeter, and subsequently he returned to Cardiff to read for an M.A. in English Literature at University College, Cardiff. He spent three years lecturing in English at Trinity and All Saints' Colleges of Education in Leeds, and since then has held the post of lecturer in English Studies at the University of Stirling. He has been a visiting lecturer in the United States, in Singapore, and in Malaya. He has published articles and reviews on Shakespeare, and is the editor of a collection of essays on *British Radio Dramatists*. At present he is working on an edition of the plays of the cavalier dramatist Shackerley Marmion, and on a study of Shakespearean dialogue.

York Notes: list of titles

CHINUA ACHEBE
A Man of the People
Arrow of God
Things Fall Apart
EDWARD ALBEE
Who's Afraid of Virginia Woolf?
ELECHI AMADI
The Concubine
ANONYMOUS
Beowulf
Everyman
AYI KWEI ARMAH
The Beautyful Ones Are Not Yet Born
W. H. AUDEN
Selected Poems
JANE AUSTEN
Emma
Mansfield Park
Northanger Abbey
Persuasion
Pride and Prejudice
Sense and Sensibility
HONORÉ DE BALZAC
Le Père Goriot
SAMUEL BECKETT
Waiting for Godot
SAUL BELLOW
Henderson, The Rain King
ARNOLD BENNETT
Anna of the Five Towns
The Card
WILLIAM BLAKE
Songs of Innocence, Songs of Experience
ROBERT BOLT
A Man For All Seasons
HAROLD BRIGHOUSE
Hobson's Choice
ANNE BRONTË
The Tenant of Wildfell Hall
CHARLOTTE BRONTË
Jane Eyre
EMILY BRONTË
Wuthering Heights
ROBERT BROWNING
Men and Women
JOHN BUCHAN
The Thirty-Nine Steps
JOHN BUNYAN
The Pilgrim's Progress
BYRON
Selected Poems
GEOFFREY CHAUCER
Prologue to the Canterbury Tales
The Clerk's Tale
The Franklin's Tale
The Knight's Tale
The Merchant's Tale
The Miller's Tale
The Nun's Priest's Tale
The Pardoner's Tale
The Wife of Bath's Tale
Troilus and Criseyde
SAMUEL TAYLOR COLERIDGE
Selected Poems
SIR ARTHUR CONAN DOYLE
The Hound of the Baskervilles

WILLIAM CONGREVE
The Way of the World
JOSEPH CONRAD
Heart of Darkness
Nostromo
Victory
STEPHEN CRANE
The Red Badge of Courage
BRUCE DAWE
Selected Poems
WALTER DE LA MARE
Selected Poems
DANIEL DEFOE
A Journal of the Plague Year
Moll Flanders
Robinson Crusoe
CHARLES DICKENS
A Tale of Two Cities
Bleak House
David Copperfield
Dombey and Son
Great Expectations
Hard Times
Little Dorrit
Oliver Twist
The Pickwick Papers
EMILY DICKINSON
Selected Poems
JOHN DONNE
Selected Poems
JOHN DRYDEN
Selected Poems
GERALD DURRELL
My Family and Other Animals
GEORGE ELIOT
Middlemarch
Silas Marner
The Mill on the Floss
T. S. ELIOT
Four Quartets
Murder in the Cathedral
Selected Poems
The Cocktail Party
The Waste Land
J. G. FARRELL
The Siege of Krishnapur
WILLIAM FAULKNER
Absalom, Absalom!
The Sound and the Fury
HENRY FIELDING
Joseph Andrews
Tom Jones
F. SCOTT FITZGERALD
Tender is the Night
The Great Gatsby
GUSTAVE FLAUBERT
Madame Bovary
E. M. FORSTER
A Passage to India
Howards End
JOHN FOWLES
The French Lieutenant's Woman
ATHOL FUGARD
Selected Plays
JOHN GALSWORTHY
Strife

MRS GASKELL
North and South

WILLIAM GOLDING
Lord of the Flies
The Spire

OLIVER GOLDSMITH
She Stoops to Conquer
The Vicar of Wakefield

ROBERT GRAVES
Goodbye to All That

GRAHAM GREENE
Brighton Rock
The Heart of the Matter
The Power and the Glory

WILLIS HALL
The Long and the Short and the Tall

THOMAS HARDY
Far from the Madding Crowd
Jude the Obscure
Selected Poems
Tess of the D'Urbervilles
The Mayor of Casterbridge
The Return of the Native
The Trumpet Major
The Woodlanders
Under the Greenwood Tree

L. P. HARTLEY
The Go-Between
The Shrimp and the Anemone

NATHANIEL HAWTHORNE
The Scarlet Letter

SEAMUS HEANEY
Selected Poems

JOSEPH HELLER
Catch-22

ERNEST HEMINGWAY
A Farewell to Arms
For Whom the Bell Tolls
The Old Man and the Sea

HERMANN HESSE
Steppenwolf

BARRY HINES
Kes

HOMER
The Iliad
The Odyssey

ANTHONY HOPE
The Prisoner of Zenda

GERARD MANLEY HOPKINS
Selected Poems

RICHARD HUGHES
A High Wind in Jamaica

TED HUGHES
Selected Poems

THOMAS HUGHES
Tom Brown's Schooldays

ALDOUS HUXLEY
Brave New World

HENRIK IBSEN
A Doll's House
Ghosts

HENRY JAMES
The Ambassadors
The Portrait of a Lady
Washington Square

SAMUEL JOHNSON
Rasselas

BEN JONSON
The Alchemist
Volpone

JAMES JOYCE
A Portrait of the Artist as a Young Man
Dubliners

JOHN KEATS
Selected Poems

PHILIP LARKIN
Selected Poems

D. H. LAWRENCE
Selected Short Stories
Sons and Lovers
The Rainbow
Women in Love

CAMARA LAYE
L'Enfant Noir

HARPER LEE
To Kill a Mocking-Bird

LAURIE LEE
Cider with Rosie

THOMAS MANN
Tonio Kröger

CHRISTOPHER MARLOWE
Doctor Faustus

ANDREW MARVELL
Selected Poems

W. SOMERSET MAUGHAM
Selected Short Stories

GAVIN MAXWELL
Ring of Bright Water

J. MEADE FALKNER
Moonfleet

HERMAN MELVILLE
Moby Dick

THOMAS MIDDLETON
Women Beware Women

THOMAS MIDDLETON *and* WILLIAM ROWLEY
The Changeling

ARTHUR MILLER
A View from the Bridge
Death of a Salesman
The Crucible

JOHN MILTON
Paradise Lost I & II
Paradise Lost IV & IX
Selected Poems

V. S. NAIPAUL
A House for Mr Biswas

ROBERT O'BRIEN
Z for Zachariah

SEAN O'CASEY
Juno and the Paycock

GABRIEL OKARA
The Voice

EUGENE O'NEILL
Mourning Becomes Electra

GEORGE ORWELL
Animal Farm
Nineteen Eighty-four

JOHN OSBORNE
Look Back in Anger

WILFRED OWEN
Selected Poems

ALAN PATON
Cry, The Beloved Country

THOMAS LOVE PEACOCK
Nightmare Abbey and *Crotchet Castle*

HAROLD PINTER
The Caretaker

SYLVIA PLATH
Selected Works

PLATO
The Republic

ALEXANDER POPE
Selected Poems

J. B. PRIESTLEY
An Inspector Calls
THOMAS PYNCHON
The Crying of Lot 49
SIR WALTER SCOTT
Ivanhoe
Quentin Durward
The Heart of Midlothian
Waverley
PETER SHAFFER
The Royal Hunt of the Sun
WILLIAM SHAKESPEARE
A Midsummer Night's Dream
Antony and Cleopatra
As You Like It
Coriolanus
Cymbeline
Hamlet
Henry IV Part I
Henry IV Part II
Henry V
Julius Caesar
King Lear
Love's Labour's Lost
Macbeth
Measure for Measure
Much Ado About Nothing
Othello
Richard II
Richard III
Romeo and Juliet
Sonnets
The Merchant of Venice
The Taming of the Shrew
The Tempest
The Winter's Tale
Troilus and Cressida
Twelfth Night
GEORGE BERNARD SHAW
Androcles and the Lion
Arms and the Man
Caesar and Cleopatra
Candida
Major Barbara
Pygmalion
Saint Joan
The Devil's Disciple
MARY SHELLEY
Frankenstein
PERCY BYSSHE SHELLEY
Selected Poems
RICHARD BRINSLEY SHERIDAN
The School for Scandal
The Rivals
R. C. SHERRIFF
Journey's End
WOLE SOYINKA
The Road
EDMUND SPENSER
The Faerie Queene (Book I)
JOHN STEINBECK
Of Mice and Men
The Grapes of Wrath
The Pearl

LAURENCE STERNE
A Sentimental Journey
Tristram Shandy
ROBERT LOUIS STEVENSON
Kidnapped
Treasure Island
TOM STOPPARD
Professional Foul
Rosencrantz and Guildenstern are Dead
JONATHAN SWIFT
Gulliver's Travels
JOHN MILLINGTON SYNGE
The Playboy of the Western World
TENNYSON
Selected Poems
W. M. THACKERAY
Vanity Fair
DYLAN THOMAS
Under Milk Wood
FLORA THOMPSON
Lark Rise to Candleford
J. R. R. TOLKIEN
The Hobbit
ANTHONY TROLLOPE
Barchester Towers
MARK TWAIN
Huckleberry Finn
Tom Sawyer
JOHN VANBRUGH
The Relapse
VIRGIL
The Aeneid
VOLTAIRE
Candide
KEITH WATERHOUSE
Billy Liar
EVELYN WAUGH
Decline and Fall
JOHN WEBSTER
The Duchess of Malfi
H. G. WELLS
The History of Mr Polly
The Invisible Man
The War of the Worlds
OSCAR WILDE
The Importance of Being Earnest
THORNTON WILDER
Our Town
TENNESSEE WILLIAMS
The Glass Menagerie
VIRGINIA WOOLF
Mrs Dalloway
To the Lighthouse
WILLIAM WORDSWORTH
Selected Poems
WILLIAM WYCHERLEY
The Country Wife
W. B. YEATS
Selected Poems